THE
HOUSE
OF LIM

•

*a study of a
Chinese farm family*

•

MARGERY WOLF

PRENTICE-HALL, INC., *Englewood Cliffs, New Jersey*

in memory of

SIDNEY MELLER

© 1968
by PRENTICE-HALL, Inc.,
Englewood Cliffs, New Jersey

30   29   28   27   26   25   24

ISBN: 0-13-394973-7

Library of Congress Catalog Card Number: 68-11211)

Printed in the United States of America

PRENTICE-HALL INTERNATIONAL, INC., *London*
PRENTICE-HALL OF AUSTRALIA, PTY. LTD., *Sydney*
PRENTICE-HALL OF CANADA, LTD., *Toronto*
PRENTICE-HALL OF INDIA PRIVATE LIMITED, *New Delhi*
PRENTICE-HALL OF JAPAN, INC., *Tokyo*

CONTENTS

PREFACE

Because my husband is an anthropologist who specializes in Chinese studies, I came in 1959 to live in a small country village in Northern Taiwan. For the next two years, home was a Chinese farm house shared with the large family of Lim. Why the Lims of Peihotien agreed to take us into their family is unclear. Our rent was certainly higher than any Taiwanese would pay, but the risk of renting to us was far greater. Many of the people in Peihotien had never seen an American before and most had never spoken to one. Our landlord, Lim Chieng-cua, evidently decided that our odd pale eyes, large noses, and unhealthy white skin did not necessarily mean we were any more unpredictable than a Taiwanese stranger. Lim Chieng-cua may have owed a social debt to the schoolmaster who introduced us to him, or he may have hoped to gain some advantage from America by sheltering its students. Perhaps he simply wished to indulge his curiosity, or perhaps he hoped that our presence in his house might in some way ease the strains that were developing within his family.

It was not until we had spent many months in the house of Lim that we began to appreciate the magnitude of our good fortune. For two generations this branch of the Lim family had held the unofficial but effective leadership of Peihotien—respected and, in some cases, feared by their fellow villagers. As guests in their home, we found we had little to fear from opportunists or thieves, for none would risk angering our mentors. We also found, however, that we had rented a certain responsibility towards the good name of the family. If we bargained so carelessly as to allow ourselves to be cheated of a few dollars, we had to a certain extent allowed the Lims to be cheated. When the village carpenter overcharged us, Lim Chieng-cua felt it necessary to retaliate with a subtle, but public, social insult. On another occasion, Lim Chieng-cua explained to us that for the sake of our good name we should eat at least one course at every village banquet to which we were invited—even if this meant attending a dozen or more banquets in a single evening. He later told our assistant that we must be urged to do this for the sake of the Lims' good name.

In time I began to refer to the Lims as "our" family, at first jokingly, but later with an odd sense of identification. I would be guilty of gross sentimentality and naive social science if I pretended that we became "members" of the Lim family. After a few months, however, the family became so used to our presence that formal expressions of politeness gave way to natural expressions, angry quarrels were not cooled by my en-trance, nor were frustrated tears removed to another room. The objec-tivity I retained toward family quarrels and factions was due more to the undeniable gulf between our two cultures and to my own timidity than to any scientific principles. The tension between Lim Chieng-cua and his elder brother's widow became to me a conflict between two good people, both of whom deserved better treatment at the hands of the other—not an abstract problem of conflicting authority in the Chinese family system. The sad life of the pretty young prostitute in our family and the behavior of her shrewish mother was personally distressing when it should have been only an excellent example of the way in which a culture with no alternatives to marriage and family handles the problem of the unmarried and the barren.

Now, some six years later and many thousand miles away, I can re-read field notes with less emotion and evaluate what happened in the house of Lim in less subjective terms. In the past year or so I have drawn together from our field data the various bits of information and inter-views we gathered from the Lims and their neighbors and combined them into a narrative. The picture of the Lim family that results is sketched by a foreigner, but the foreigner has tried not to attach American motiva-tions to Taiwanese behavior. Of necessity the ordering of some events and the effect these events had on some lives is based on my conjecture. I have, I hope, made it apparent to the reader when I am guessing about something and when I have been told about it—and for that matter, when I doubt the validity of what I have been told. All the quotations are translations of comments made by family members, their neighbors, and their relatives. With many members of the family my communication was clumsy because of my and their weakness in Mandarin (the official language of China) and my total lack of Hokkien (the local Chinese dialect). Fortunately, my assistant, a girl who grew up in a similar village, developed during her work with us the invaluable capacity to interpret without seeming to be a part of the conversation. She had, moreover, a phenomenal memory that enabled her to recall as much as fifteen minutes of conversation verbatim and to render the content of interviews many times that length. Without her, many of the more detailed conversations would never have been recorded. Her talents extended beyond those of the inconspicuous interpreter and ambulatory tape-recorder. Her capacity to appear unimportant but sympathetic made her the confidante of many and, for me, a library of information about local attitudes toward people and their lives.

I am not an anthropologist, but this book has benefited from several careful readings by an anthropologist who knows the Lims as well as I. In the pages that follow I have tried to do three things: to present a case study for the social scientist interested in the strains inherent to the form of family considered ideal in China, to provide another account of village life for those with a more general interest in China, and to tell a good story. I have depended heavily upon my husband's advice as to the information important to a case study, made my own judgements as to what might interest the general reader about life in a Taiwanese village, and left the story to the Lims.

Books such as Ida Pruitt's *Daughter of Han* and Lin Yueh-hwa's *The Golden Wing* have made major contributions to our understanding of China. It is, after all, the nameless and the unimportant who make up the society over which leaders and politicians debate. The statesmen may control a country's temporal fate, but its existence over time depends upon the farmer, the peddler, the noodle-maker. China's history over the centuries has varied with the strength of its leaders, but its people have gone on being Chinese, whoever the ruler, whatever the political crises. I hope that in some small way this study of an unimportant family may add to our understanding of what being Chinese is all about.

On every page of this book there is evidence of the debt I owe the people of Peihotien, both Lims and non-Lims. Less apparent is the contribution of our field staff, but their patience, endurance, and plain hard work will always be remembered with gratitude. This includes the small dragon who ruled our kitchen, balanced our budget, corrected our table manners, and sewed on our buttons. My husband, Arthur Wolf, deserves more than thanks. Without him, there would have been no House of Lim—unless he had written it himself. Thanks are due to many people who read and criticized early drafts, in particular: Mrs. Pi-yung Hsu who spent many hours selecting authentic, even though fictitious, Taiwanese names; Mrs. Sidney Meller for the difficult reading of a first draft; and Dr. Arthur Vidich for his many valuable suggestions. I am also indebted to the Cornell committee of the London–Cornell Project for the funds they made available to me for secretarial help.

M.W.

FOREWORD

I shall not disguise my pleasure in being able, by writing a foreword to this admirable book, to contradict its author. Mrs. Wolf tells us in her preface that she is not an anthropologist and goes on to set out her three aims: to offer us a case study of a large Chinese family; to "provide another account of village life for those with a general interest in China"; and to "tell a good story." The charming simplicity and modesty of these brief statements may seduce the unwary reader into believing that the ease with which the subsequent narrative flows has been the happy result of literary skill coming upon a ready-made story. If anybody closes this book thinking that it is the Lims who have enlightened and entertained him, he will (I suspect) have fallen into a trap cunningly laid for him by the author. It is my job to put him on his guard and to force him to pay Mrs. Wolf the tribute that she seems unwilling to claim for herself.

This is a very cleverly constructed book in which the facts—so far from speaking for themselves—are made eloquent by the ideas which inspired their collection and arrangement. Of course, if Mrs. Wolf insists that she is not an anthropologist, then we must respect her disavowal. (It is perhaps a sign of the times. In the good old days people had less respect for professional degrees and licenses to practice.) I think it is all the more necessary for me to show how important anthropology has been both in her choice of problems and in the methods she has used to study them. I shall come back to the problems; let me say a word on methods.

Professor and Mrs. Wolf lived for two years in the household described in this book. In that period, while they were engaged in the investigation of many aspects of village life, they had the opportunity to study their immediate hosts and friends at close quarters. The word "study" may chill some readers, especially if they think of themselves as being in the position of the Lims and wonder how they would feel if their domestic life, quarrels and all, were under the cool gaze of foreign observers. But anthropology is a science in which the common humanity of the observer and the observed does not allow the one to make an object of the other. The investigator and the investigated are in a social relationship; and it follows that the facts about those under study must

not only be checked and checked again for their accuracy (as in any kind
of systematic inquiry), but must also be set out in such a manner as to
be consistent with the duty of frankness that the student owes to his
readers and the obligations of loyalty and friendship he bears to his
subjects. Anthropology studies people intensively and decently, and I am
sure that Mrs. Wolf has discharged her double duty in a way that will
command the respect of the most experienced practitioners of the craft.
The care and intensiveness of the observations are matched by the
delicacy and sensitivity of their expression.

Sentimentality is the enemy of anthropology. To write with understanding of people whose institutions and beliefs are alien requires the
anthropologist to make an effort to see them as they are and to portray
them as he sees them. He must view them in the round and strive to
penetrate the meaning of their behavior through the language they use.
Because they are his fellow human beings the anthropologist has priv-
ileged access to them; but because they speak a different language and
think with different symbols, he has to break the code of another culture.
To make us the beneficiaries of his studies, he must translate the exotic
idiom into a language we follow, but he must do his best to avoid distorting his findings in the process of translation. Mrs. Wolf's book is in
elegant English, yet she is not acting as, so to say, a simultaneous trans-
lator, but rather as a creative interpreter. She has seized in this book
on one segment of Chinese life, extracted its order and meaning, and
made us the fortunate heirs of her understanding.

The Lims of this study are Taiwanese, and, except in her subtitle
and preface, Mrs. Wolf talks about Taiwan, not China in general. I
must respect her choice of terms, but I should not be doing my job
competently if I failed to point out that we may sometimes be misled by
her terminology. Two phases of modern history (accidents from our
present sociological viewpoint) may tempt us to think of Taiwan as a
separate "country." From 1895 to 1945 it was governed by the Japanese;
since 1949 it has been cut off by civil war from the mainland of China.
But it is part of China, and nobody familiar with Chinese patterns of
social organization and behavior will have any difficulty in recognizing
the Lims and their neighbors as good Chinese. True, their mother tongue
is not Mandarin, but then they share this peculiarity with millions of
Chinese on the mainland.

The point is worth stressing because there is a tendency to look upon
studies made in Taiwan (and in the British colony of Hong Kong) as

though they were in some derogatory sense peripheral. Naturally, it is frustrating for social scientists interested in China to be held off from the mainland; and there is a certain unpleasant irony in the fact that there are now many more North American and European anthropologists and sociologists equipped and eager to study Chinese society than there were before 1949. Yet, as *The House of Lim* decisively demonstrates, field studies of crucial importance can be made in Taiwan; and I could adduce similar evidence for a parallel statement on Hong Kong. Professor and Mrs. Wolf were accompanied in Taiwan by other American field workers, and they have been succeeded by yet others. (I am happy to say that a British student has been added to the ranks of anthropologists to whom Taiwanese hospitality has been extended.) The research work carried out in recent years in both Taiwan and Hong Kong has brought China fully within the range of the societies now being systematically examined in the light of the problems and techniques of modern social science.

The House of Lim touches on many aspects of village life—agriculture, business, religion, youth organization (note especially the remarks on *lo mua*), kinship, sex (the accounts of prostitution are incisive), and so on. But the book is above all the study of a family. Now, it may seem to some readers that the Chinese family is a well-worn theme. Many books and learned papers have been written on it, by both Chinese and foreigners, and the "large" Chinese family has been a familiar piece of furniture in the minds of several generations of Western intellectuals. Let the reader beware: the study of the Chinese family is a never-ending enterprise, and he must be ready to revise his ideas on it as research of increasing sophistication is put before him. He will find in this book an epitome of the most modern knowledge of the Chinese family in its traditional form.

The Lims, when the Wolfs lived with them, were a "large" family. In this they were both typical and untypical of their society. They were typical of its ideals and untypical of its realities. It is not an accident that (with one exception) they were the only family of its kind in Peihotien, and the richest. Bigness is a matter for pride, and those who would maintain it must struggle, as Mrs. Wolf shows us, against the forces that press relentlessly for its undoing. For it is not crude numerical size that characterizes a family of this sort; it is its complexity. And from the complexity flow the problems which Mrs. Wolf's narrative illustrates clearly and abundantly.

The Chinese family normally recruits itself through its sons, its daughters being exchanged for daughters-in-law. Each new marriage brings into the house a focus of dissension, for the new small family which it creates within the bosom of the greater family gradually matures into an independent unit. Some greater families dissolve when their sons are married; virtually all disappear by the time the old father dies, for then, as Mrs. Wolf tells us for the village of Peihotien, the wives of the brothers allow their interests in their own small families to issue in quarrels. If, that is to say, a family has two or more sons, the normal unfolding of the cycle of development sees them become husbands and fathers only to make them move on to form separate units.

But occasionally a large family for a time escapes this fate. The Lim family was such a one. The potential new families within it were not realized. Lim Chieng-cua together with his wife and children remained along with his older brother's widow and descendants in an undivided family. It is important to remember that every Chinese family, be it simple or complex, holds a joint estate under the management of the senior male (or, in some cases, a widow). When, as in the house of Lim, the estate is valuable and economically differentiated into agricultural and business sectors, it can be efficiently and profitably run by the specialized work of different branches of the family. But the very econ-omic features which make the estate productive are also the foe of family unity. Each son being endowed at birth (or adoption) with a right to an equal (or nearly equal) share in the estate on its division, jealousies can easily arise between brothers and between their respective smaller fam-ilies over the differential enjoyment of the fruits of the undivided estate. The agricultural half of such a large family may suspect that the business half is taking more out of the total estate than its arithmetical share justifies. In Mrs. Wolf's account of the Lims we can see these suspicions in action.

It may well be significant that of the two brothers, Lim Chieng-cua and Lim Hue-lieng, one is dead. A-pou, the latter's widow, represents her late husband's interests in the family. "When," Mrs. Wolf writes, "Lim Chieng-cua makes a decision affecting the welfare of the family, he is obliged to consult her." Her relations with Chieng-cua can be seen to express the tension between the main component units of the family. But (we may suspect) it is precisely because Hue-lieng is dead and only one man is left in the senior generation that the house of Lim is a house long undivided. I should suggest (without foisting my opinion on Mrs. Wolf) that, while the quarrels precipitated by women are often seen as the major causes of the disruption of Chinese families, it is to the brittle relationship between brothers that we must look for an understanding of why, in spite of the great pride taken in large families, they are none- theless very rare. And in this connection it is worth glancing at the other large family in Peihotien. It consists of "a pair of surprisingly amiable brothers, both of whom work out of the village at well-paid jobs, leaving their two wives, ten children, unmarried sister, and mother in an ample village home. The two wives are so alike they could be sisters and they work together in effortless cooperation." Perhaps the wives are in har- mony because the husbands are away from home.

The difficulties inherent in the fraternal relationship in China are illuminated by another aspect of this book. I have stressed the role of anthropology in it, but in fact Mrs. Wolf also writes from a psychological point of view, and her comments on the training of children show us, among other things, that the role of brother is so modified by the age of the incumbent that it presents a problem to those who must perform it. When brothers are children, the older must give way to the younger. When they are grown up, the younger must defer to the older. So that the tensions promoted by the rivalries built into the fraternal relation- ship would appear to be aggravated by the contradictory nature of the expectations aroused about the way in which brothers should ideally behave.

All these are major problems in the study of China, and what Mrs. Wolf says about Peihotien can be generalized to help us in our analysis of the family institutions of the country as a whole. No reader who is familiar with Chinese society will have any difficulty in making the jump from the particular to the general. But there is one matter dealt with in the book that, seeming to be peculiar to Taiwan, may appear to be inapt for generalization. Mrs. Wolf tells us that in the generation of Lim Chieng-cua's father nearly half the men in Peihotien married *simpua,* that is to say, little girls brought into the house in prospect of marriage to its sons. As "little daughters-in-law," *simpua* are given parents-in-law before they have husbands. Yet the institution is in fact known very widely in China, and it is only its extensive use in Taiwan that sets that island apart. Because the practice is to be found throughout China, we can profit from the analysis which Mrs. Wolf is able to make where the data are abundant. I suggest that we ought to pay particular attention to what she says about the sexual maladjustment to which *simpua* marriage seems to give rise (boy and girl having been reared as though they were brother and sister) and about the declining viability of the institution in conditions where parents can no longer so decisively dictate the choice of marriage partners.

The material brought back from Peihotien by Professor and Mrs. Wolf is (as I can testify from my private knowledge of it) one of the treasures of the ethnography of China. As readers of this book we are afforded the opportunity to see the data on one family assembled to make both a case study and a story. The case study is no less literature than the story, and the story is not a whit less anthropological for being marvelously told. I shall risk being charged with greediness by saying that I hope that *The House of Lim* is merely the first of a long series of books to come from the study of Peihotien. That village is now an important feature of the scholar's map of China.

MAURICE FREEDMAN
*London School of Economics and
Political Science*

PEOPLE AND PLACES

All of the surnames and personal names in this book are pseudonyms. They are written according to Chinese custom: surname preceding personal names. All names except for the one man who was born on the mainland of China are Hokkïen and are romanized according to the system devised by Nicholas C. Bodman in his text, *Spoken Amoy Hokkien* (Charles Grenier & Son Ltd., Kuala Lumpur, 1955). Tone marks and other linguistic devices have been omitted.

Place names other than that of Taiwan and its major cities are also fictitious. They are written in a standard romanization of Mandarin, using the post office spelling now customary among students of China.

THE PLACES

Chuanchou	A district in Fukien from which the Lim family migrated
Hotien	The district in which Peihotien is located
Lungyen	A small city near Peihotien
Nanhotien	Another village in the Hotien district
Peihotien	The village in which the Lim family lives
Tainan	A large city in the southern part of the island
Taipei	Capital of Taiwan
Tapu	The market town which serves Peihotien
Tungan	A section of the Chuanchou district in Fukien

THE PEOPLE

Chang Jong-kuei	A mainlander, married to Gioq-ki
Iu Mui-mue	Lim Han-ci's third adopted daughter; adopted to marry Lim Chieng-cua but did not do so
Lau Bit	Daughter of Lau Kim-chiok, Lim Chieng-cua's former mistress
Lau Kim-chiok	Mistress of Lim Chieng-cua

Li Guat-ngo	Adopted daughter of Lim A-pou
Lim A-bok	First born son of Lim Hue-lieng and his adopted sister, A-pou
Lim A-hua	Adopted daughter of Lim Hue-lieng and his second wife, So-lan
Lim A-ki	Wife of A-bok
Lim A-pou	Lim Han-ci's first adopted daughter; wife of Lim Hue-lieng
Lim Bieng-cu	Second daughter, fifth child of Lim Chieng-cua and his wife, Chui-ieng
Lim Chieng-cua	Second son of Lim Han-ci; present head of the house of Lim
Lim Chui-ieng	Wife of Lim Chieng-cua
Lim Cin-hok	Fourth son, sixth child of Lim Chieng-cua and his wife, Chui-ieng
Lim Gioq-ki	Oldest daughter of Lim Hue-lieng and his second wife, So-lan; only child born to them
Lim Han-ci	The father
Lim Hue-lieng	Eldest son of Lim Han-ci
Lim Kim-hok	First born son of Lim Chieng-cua and his wife, Chui-ieng
Lim Kui-hok	Third son, fourth child of Lim Chieng-cua and his wife, Chui-ieng
Lim Le-cu	First daughter, second child of Lim Chieng-cua and his wife, Chui-ieng
Lim Masa	Second son of Lim Hue-lieng and his adopted sister, A-pou
Lim So-lan	Second wife of Lim Hue-lieng
Lim Thiam-hok	Second son, third child of Lim Chieng-cua and his wife, Chui-ieng
Ng Kok-hua	Son of Ng Kui-lian; proprietor of Peihotien's store
Ng Kui-lian	Go-between for marriage of Lim Chieng-cua and Chui-ieng
Tan A-hong	Lim Han-ci's second adopted daughter who was re-sold when his own daughter was returned
Tan Chai-ngo	Second-born daughter of Tan A-hong
Tan Chun-ieng	First-born daughter of Tan A-hong

chapter 1

THE
CITY
AND THE
MARKET TOWN

Taiwan is a beautiful green island, 240 miles long and 88 miles wide. On the east coast the mountains rise straight from the sea to over 13,000 feet. Stretches of the one-lane highway connecting north and south are literally carved out of cliffs that hang above the Pacific. The mountains, a steep, tangled mass of rich tropical foliage and giant trees, appear uninhabitable and uninhabited, but the remnants of nine different aborigine groups somehow manage a living on their precipitous slopes. In the west the mountains descend less dramatically onto a fertile plain that extends to the sea. It is on the rich, alluvial soils of this plain that the majority of the twelve million Chinese inhabitants make their home. Nearly every tillable foot of land is sectioned and under cultivation. In the north, where the dry season is limited to a few weeks in the fall, the land is a patchwork of neatly squared and banked rice paddies. On a sunny day the intensity of the green in a paddy of young growing rice plants is almost painful; even on the dull, humid days of summer the green seems to rise in the steaming air, distorting colors into complements. Farther south, where the dry season is longer, the color is more subdued, both because wet paddy farming is less common and because the foliage is not washed by a daily rain.

The capital of Taiwan, Taipei, sits in a damp basin on the northern tip of the plain. People who have lived in Peiping and Nanking say it is an ugly city, lacking the beauty of cities on the Chinese mainland but retaining all their faults. Since much of its growth took place during the fifty-odd years of Japanese administration, Taipei is weighted down with ugly though solid Japanese colonial architecture, studious imitations of public buildings in the British colonies. Current shoddy attempts at sinification make them even less attractive. In some of the more expensive residential neighborhoods there are still beautiful examples of Japanese domestic architecture hidden behind high brick walls. These residential streets, many of them unpaved and all bordered by open sewer ditches, are peaceful, the quiet disturbed only by an occasional car, a squeaking pedi-cab, and the varied, melodic calls of passing peddlers, knife-sharpeners, and shoe-repairers. At night the soft clack-clack of the blind masseur's bamboo rattle is as natural as a bird's song.

The streets in the business section of the city are anything but peaceful. The great clattering, rattling buses seem to have no springs and no speed limits; automobiles, mainly in the form of taxis or military jeeps, use horns more frequently than brakes. Sidewalks and roadways alike are clogged with bicycles, pedi-cabs, and pedestrians who reverse direction, cut across traffic, or come to a complete halt without warning or apparent reason. Cartloads of bricks and logs drawn by sweating, straining men or ambling yellow oxen use the same lanes as buses hurtling forward at forty miles an hour.

Beyond the hustling downtown districts that sell the essential luxuries to the wealthy are the Taiwanese sections of the city, areas of commerce and residence, often combined, that seem both flimsy and timeless. There is architecture here too, but it would take a coldly disciplined observer to look above the busy life in the shops and the streets to evaluate the style of the buildings. Here is the real texture of a Chinese city. There is poverty, but not the thin, sour smell of poverty in American cities. Tiny shops sell cheap, shoddy cotton goods, coarse household basketry, and thin metal pots and pans. The owners' wives squat in front, fanning portable stoves of clay and coal dust, cooking the evening meal of vegetables and pork fat or, depending upon the day's business, only vegetables. Customers step over and around the children sleeping or playing amid the merchandise and on the sidewalks; they bargain with the shopkeeper's wife while the baby tied on her back sleeps peacefully through their rising and falling voices. Few cars attempt the narrow lanes but pedi-cabs and bicycles thread in and around the pedestrians with a grace and speed that often ends in a squealing of brakes and shouted oaths. In the few arcades or streets closed to automobiles in the United States and England, one is conscious of the sound of feet on concrete, but in Taipei, even though the wooden clogs of the poor make much more noise than Western leather, one is conscious of voices. Children cry, women gossip, store-keepers greet friends and customers, peddlers inform passers-by of the quality and freshness of their wares, pedi-cab drivers shout warnings to pedestrians about to step in front of them, neighbors discuss the bargains they've found, and not infrequently family quarrels are presented for the world to judge. Winter or summer, day or night, there is always the smell of smoke—coal smoke, charcoal smoke, fuel oil. Often it is delicately embroidered with a thread of incense coming from a family altar in the back of a store or from a small temple tucked down a side alley. The air is heavy with smells, not just smoke, but the oily smells of cooking, the salty smell of drying fish, the sharp tang of pickled vegetables, the elegant smell of sandalwood being fashioned into boxes and furnishings for the rich, and always some-where in every neighborhood the smell of the "honey-wagon," a slow moving tank cart that goes from house to house to collect "night-soil."

In 1957 my husband and I arrived in Taipei and spent the better part of a year there, studying Mandarin. The following year, the majority of which I was forced to spend in the United States because of the illnesses of my parents, my husband searched the island for a suitable village in which to carry out the anthropological field project that had brought him to Taiwan. I returned not to the noisy, jostling city but to a small, quiet village on the banks of the Tamsui River. In its way of life, Peihotien was far from Taipei; in miles, the distance was not great. With luck and a feeling of urgency, the trip from the Taipei train station to our doorstep could be made in an hour, half by train and half by foot. The train rumbled through Taipei suburbs, a small city, a couple of small market towns, and much open paddy land before it dropped us in the market town of Tapu. Tapu is the buying, selling, repairing, and general servicing town for a number of villages, including the one in which I was to live.

The Tapu train station opens onto a little square; the square in turn opens onto the main street of the town. I have never seen the square completely empty, not even in the heavy rains that break the heat of summer afternoons. There is a man who sells hot noodles from a little cart, another with fresh fruit, another with newspapers

and gaudy magazines. There is often an itinerant peddler or two during the afternoons, keeping up a steady stream of jokes and praise for
his merchandise that would win approval from any sideshow barker.
And evenings, particularly the warm, humid evenings of summer
when houses are empty and life moves to the doorsteps and walkways,
there are elaborate traveling medicine shows with magicians, or acro-
bats, or strongmen, or even modest operas. On those nights it is
difficult to pass through the crowds, and the foreigner's white face
isn't half as interesting as the antics going on under the bare electric
light bulb that serves as the peddler's spotlight.

The remainder of the trip to Peihotien is on foot. There are
always a few pedi-cabs by the station, but one ride in an aged pedi-cab
down a rutted country path is sufficient to discourage a second. The
walk across Tapu down its main street shouldn't take more than two
or three minutes but it usually took me much longer. One side of the
street is a roofed colonnade, protecting the shopper from the heat of
the sun and the drenching of the rains. Here are the more substantial
merchants of Tapu, the men who don't rent rickety stalls or push-
carts but own or lease stores with sleeping rooms above or in the back
for their families. Although there is a Western-style pharmacy in
Tapu, as gaudy and cluttered as any American drug store, the old-
fashioned Chinese medicine shop still does a better business. My husband often stopped there to talk with the druggist, an intelligent man
who enjoys conversation, while I admired the rows of dignified crock-
ery containers unsullied by advertising. Even on the hottest days the
dim interior is cool and exotically fragrant. Next door is something
that might be called a housewares store. From the open front to the
dark, dusty back, the ceiling is festooned with the merchant's wares—
bunches of brass tea kettles looking like giant clusters of pale grapes,
chains of shallow, disc-shaped frying pans, strings of short-handled
rice-stalk brooms, and ropes of household brushes. Stacked from floor
to ceiling are baskets for straining, baskets for carrying, baskets for
drying, baskets for fishing, baskets for storing. A shaky tower of
pointed bamboo hats that serve the farmer as both umbrella and
sunshade perch on an old wooden counter. Hanging from rusty nails
are a collection of razor-sharp cleavers that function in the Chinese
kitchen both as paring knife and butcher knife; there are dishes, cheap
and easily broken; there are small tin cooking stoves that on careful
examination prove to be ingeniously constructed of flattened beer

cans salvaged from the garbage dumps of American military installa-
tions. In the next store a pall of dust hangs on everything. This is a
small coal-kerosene-rice store, and the debris from the hand-operated
rice polishing mill makes everything, even the black coal, a shade
lighter. Toward the back there are baskets of charcoal and bundles of
neatly cut twigs and branches, carefully graded and tied. Against the
back wall are stacked bottles of wine and beer, their necks entwined
with cheap handmade rope. The piquant, not quite fresh smell in the
air comes from next door, the store we called the pickle shop for want of
a better name. Huge jars of pickles—pickled cabbage, pickled rad-
dishes, pickled eggplants, even pickled eggs—fill the front of the store,
the more expensive delicacies displayed in glass jars, the more routine
in heavy, waist-high earthenware crocks. Only a few are preserved in
vinegar. Most are salted and allowed to season for several months, or
dried in the hot, baking summer sun, or soaked in soy sauce, herbs, or
wine. The unlighted rear of the store is brightened somewhat by the
gaudy labels on a few shelves of canned foods. They are expensive,
not as tasty as the local product, and often dangerous with age and
contamination. Nearer the front are the precious tins of powdered
milk, a mother's only solution to a dry breast in this damp climate
where dairy cows quickly succumb to tuberculosis.

The heart of the town, or at least the source of the greatest
commotion each forenoon, is the roofed food market. The market
would be difficult to locate were it not for the overflow of shoppers
and farmers. The entrance is little more than a narrow alley between
two store-fronts, an alley made even narrower by the half dozen farmers squatting there amid their baskets of produce. These are men who
can't afford to rent stalls under the protection of the roof or farmers
who happen that day to have some surplus vegetables or a sudden
shortage of cash. Just a few steps down the alley is the open market
shed itself and what seems to be a disorganized profusion of produce
heaped on trays, piled in baskets, spread on tables, or simply stacked
on the bare packed earth: fresh onions, cucumbers, garlic, an infinite
variety of melons and squash, eggplants, bamboo shoots, and occasionally fresh mushrooms brought in by some enterprising merchant
with Taipei contacts. Scattered between and on top of the vegetables
are bananas, papayas, pineapples, guavas, and a few precious apples
imported from Japan. Adding a sinister note to the confusion of produce are the meatstalls with carcasses of pigs hanging on huge hooks,

great hunks of snowy fat (the poor man's meat), buckets of blood and entrails. The fish stalls, less gory and less colorful, abound with local river fish and a few ocean fish brought in on the early train, some swimming in buckets, others gutted but missing no eyes—a great deli- cacy, or tails—a matter of aesthetics. And everywhere there are chickens, ducks, geese, both live and dead. The smells to a foreign nose are sometimes exhilirating, sometimes appalling; the sounds are bewildering. The day's fowl quack, cluck, and honk their distress; above their protest the voices of customers and merchants rise and fall. The din of heated bargaining blends a variety of languages. The farmers speak either Hokkien or Hakka, the native Chinese dialects of the island; a few merchants and their friends converse in Japanese; policemen and soldiers prefer Mandarin, the official language.

Away from the uproar of the market, Tapu's streets seem rela- tively calm. The paved main street ends at the canal, an irrigation ditch civilized by concrete banks for its passage through town. In several places, steps that lead into the canal end in small platforms where the storekeepers' wives and daughters can do their laundry while keeping an eye on the store. There are more shops on both sides of the canal: a small bookstore, a tailor, a fabric and ready-made clothing store, a photographer, and a paper store that supplies school children with copy books and pencils, and adults with the paraphernalia of worship— metal wires dipped in incense and bundles of spirit money burned to provide for the deceased. One of my favorite shops is that of the *beidz-* maker who fills the air with a lively rhythmic chwing-chwing sound as he fluffs cotton into puffy battings for warm winter comforters. A little farther down the street a noodle-maker is usually at work. He sus- pends strips of dough between pegged poles which he gradually moves farther and farther apart as the noodles stretch and dry. Just beyond the noodle-maker is a small, paved square, formed where the canal goes underground. This is the site of a shrine dedicated to Tu Ti Kung, the lowest ranking god in the Chinese supernatural bureauc- racy. Tu Ti Kung serves his celestial superiors as the official recorder of the activities of the living. In the country, he is the guardian of the land and the god of agriculture; in the town, he is considered a patron of business and a god of wealth. The responsibility for burning in- cense at his shrine each morning rotates among the families residing in his district.

Across the square a narrow, unpaved alley twists past a coffin shop, smelling incongruously fresh and spring-like from the fragrant sandalwood; it makes another turn at the legless fortune teller's shop, passes a few houses, and abruptly disappears in the open, shimmering rice paddies.

chapter 2

THE
VILLAGE

Passing out of the narrow lane into the open countryside is like passing through the gates of a walled city. The backs of the tall, window-
less brick houses form a solid barrier between the noise of the town
and the stillness of the country. The shouts of street hawkers and the
loud inquiries of customers are softened to a murmur. The senses are
now more impressed by what is seen than by what is heard. In the
distance the mountains limit the eyes' sweep. Even the thick anarchy
of ferns and trees and vines does not relieve their harsh, jagged lines.
But, on a hot day, as the humidity builds up, the mountains recede,
become vague and indistinct, the misty impressions of an old Chinese
scroll. An uneven line of shrubs and trees, darker in color, more
precise in outline, seems to be at the base of the mountains but
actually is several miles closer, hugging the damp banks of the Tamsui
River, sheltering the village of Peihotien. This area on which Tapu
turns its back is known as Hotien.

Although there are now many surnames represented in Hotien, the
district was originally settled by the Lim family. The Chinese record
the births, marriages, and deaths of their male progeny in genealogies,
thus providing a skeletal history of their lineage. To them, the important part of the document is the long family tree which traces their
line of descent back through many centuries, but in most genealogies
there is also a short essay describing the family's place of origin, the
location of the clan temple that houses the memorial tablets of more
distant ancestors, and perhaps even some sketches of the temple itself.
It is from a document of this kind and from rambling conversations
with the elderly men and women of Peihotien that I obtained the

mythical-historical background of the Lim family with whom we lived.

As with nearly all of the ancestors of the Hokkien-speaking residents of Taiwan, the Lims' ancestors were born in the province of Fukien. Around 1770, two Lim brothers left their village in the Tungan district of Chuanchou and migrated to Taiwan, lured by the prospect of free virgin land. After looking around a bit, they settled along the Tamsui River and began to till the soil. Evidently they prospered, for their descendants were numerous. Every few years a member of the group went back to Chuanchou to pay their respects to the ancestors in the lineage temple in Fukien and to record in the family genealogy the recent deaths and births in Taiwan. The trip was not an easy one and after several generations the Taiwan branch of the family began to feel less closely allied to the family in their old home. At last a representative was sent to make a copy of the old genealogy in Chuanchou and bring it to Taiwan. From then on, only the names of the descendants of the two Lim brothers who migrated to Taiwan were entered in the genealogy. Until the middle of the nineteenth century, the Lims of Hotien were a strong and united group. Some of the family units were more successful than others, but even the landless families who worked as tenants under their more fortunate kinsmen shared in the profits from the portion of land owned jointly by all Lims. The proceeds from this corporate land were used to finance various activities, not the least of which was a huge feast at the annual meeting.

Toward the end of the nineteenth century, the lineage organization of the Lims began to disintegrate, splintering along the lines of the main family branches. Often the dissolution of large lineages such as the Lims follows disagreements over the management of the joint land holdings or suspicion of malfeasance in the disposition of their profits. Whatever the cause in the Lim family, the elders of the dissident branches once again copied the original genealogy and from that time forward entered only the names of the descendants of their own branch.

Just when and in what order these events took place in the district of Hotien is subject to question. The elderly, the men and women in their 70's, are the people who have both the time and the interest to speculate about the past. They share with all men the desire to tell the way it ought to have been rather than the way it was, to simplify rather than to complicate. Often their interpretations are devised from half-remembered stories of their own aged parents and grandparents. According to the residents of Hotien, the district is comprised of four distinct areas. The most common explanation for these sections is that they reflect the settlement pattern of the five branches of the Lim lineage when it disintegrated, two of the branches living so close together that they formed a single section. This explanation has some validity. Although all are related, the Lims within each area are more closely related to each other than they are to the Lims in adjoining areas. The four sections are inhabited by clusters of kinsmen bound together by ties of common descent. In earlier years when the nearby hills still posed a threat of bandits, kinsmen collected together for mutual protection, but even now few families consider building at any great distance from their relatives. A family in need of additional living space usually adds to the old family home or builds a new structure next door. The bonds of kinship alone are enough to create a sense of community.

While the Lim clan was breaking apart, families of other surnames were moving into the areas, building homes on the edges of the Lim villages and buying land from Lim families who for one reason or another came upon bad times. The influx of other surnames occurred too late in the settlement of the Hotien area, however, for them to challenge the dominance of the Lims. An Ong family in Peihotien has lived there for nearly a hundred years, but they are nonetheless outsiders in a Lim village and still are referred to amusingly as "newcomers." A Chinese other than a Lim suffers from no discriminatory practices in Peihotien, but he always feels a certain uneasiness when he notes that about every third person his neighbor meets is a relative while he himself may not run across a single relation, regardless of how many trusted friends cross his path.

With each new colonial administration or reform movement on Taiwan the Hotien area has been divided and recombined into different administrative districts. It is not surprising that the residents of the area have come to ignore the official districts, accepting as inevitable that the office to which they went last year to pay their taxes will impatiently direct them elsewhere this year. Their religious organization and social affairs are conducted within the boundaries that have historical significance for some and permanence for all, the four areas that grew out of the division of the Lim descent group generations ago. I doubt that the more recent arrivals in Peihotien are even aware of the origin of the cooperation between the four areas. Although it is apparent to the least observant that the area is dominated by Lims, the exclusiveness found in clan villages in mainland China does not exist here. The ties which connect the four villages of Hotien more closely to each other than to the surrounding villages are not questioned, nor are the rights and obligations of those within the district, regardless of surname. The temple in the center of Hotien is supported by all four areas and though the list of donors is dominated by the name Lim, it is in no sense a Lim temple. When it was Peihotien's turn to cleanse the gods of the temple by carrying them across a bed of hot coals, the carriers were not limited to Lims but to residents of Peihotien village.

In many ways this temple, the home of Shang Ti Kung, is a focal point for the district of Hotien. During my stay in the area the villagers spent a great deal of time and money in totally refurbishing the temple, and celebrated its completion in a three-day festival of rededication. Shang Ti Kung is responsible for the district of Hotien in much the same way as the Mandarins of old were responsible for particular districts. Once each year he is placed on a sedan chair and carried through the four sections of his district on a tour of inspection. The sound of cymbals and firecrackers punctuates his progress and along the way his subjects greet him with bows and incense, mingling prayers and offerings. During the rest of the year he stays in his temple where he is visited daily by villagers seeking advice and help. Shang Ti Kung can cure a sick pig, raise the price of rice, discipline an unmanageable daughter-in-law, make a barren woman fertile. He is not obliged to provide these services, but if approached with respect and handsomely bribed, he might.

While Shang Ti Kung influences the welfare of the entire district of Hotien, his underling, Tu Ti Kung, is associated with smaller areas, the villages. To one side of the main path into Peihotien there is a magnificent old tree, thick of trunk and limb. Beneath it is a small stone shrine, the home of Peihotien's Tu Ti Kung. Although he lacks Shang Ti Kung's influence in heaven, Tu Ti Kung is a valuable intermediary. He passes on complaints about local conditions and makes decisions about where and when new buildings may be constructed and old ones torn down. He is the scribe and recorder for the supernatural bureaucracy; to him the villagers must report each birth, death, and marriage. In Tapu, Tu Ti Kung is the patron of the business establishments in his neighborhood. In Peihotien, he watches over the village farmers.

Peihotien is by far the most attractive of the villages of Hotien. The others have become dusty tangles of buildings in a maze of narrow paths. Unwilling to give up the precious paddy land for anything so unprofitable as living space, the growing population has built new wings and even new houses in courtyards and passageways, destroying trees and shrubs that once gave grace to their setting. Few houses enjoy the filtered shade of old trees, and the scraggly bushes scattered among them are so frequently attacked by animals and children that their life expectancy is short. Peihotien's site on the bank of the Tamsui is, by comparison, luxuriant in large healthy trees and a variety of smaller greenery. In the days when the area was settled, long before modern truck farming, the thin, sandy soil appeared useless, fit only for building sites, kitchen gardens, and drying grounds. Peihotien has grown as rapidly as its neighbors, but there is still an unusual amount of space between houses. Several families make use of it by maintaining bamboo groves, adding tender bamboo shoots to their diet and another source of shade and texture to their landscape. Even in the dry days after the rice harvest when hot winds carry the dust from the drained paddies high into the air, Peihotien seems more protected, cooler, cleaner. From a distance the other villages of Hotien can readily be identified for what they are, but Peihotien is a pleasant uncertainty, a clump of dark green foliage with a suggestion of rose brick and a glimpse of the soaring lines of a rich tile roof.

Before 1920, when the railroad was laid through Tapu, Peihotien's location on the Tamsui River had more than aesthetic value. The river, as a major thoroughfare, was important to the economy of the village. Two or three families supplemented their farm income by poling ferries across the river and several village men supported their families by transporting goods between the remote villages and Taipei. Peihotien was an agricultural village, but its farmers depended upon the river to tide them over when crops failed or families became too large. The advent of the railroad with its faster, more comfortable transportation soon ended river travel and the advantage of Peihotien's position beside it. Before long the railroad took the river's place in the village's economy, and then some. It was less than a half hour's walk from Peihotien to the railway station in Tapu and only a few more minutes by train to the factories in other cities.

Moreover, efficient transportation brought some light industry to Tapu itself. Instead of working with their fathers on the land as they had for centuries, young men began going to the factories. The wages they brought home often made the difference between having just enough to eat and having plenty to eat. Few farmers sold their land or gave up farming, but by 1960, nearly every family had at least one member working outside the village for a cash income to supplement the seasonal income from the land.

During the period in which they were building the railroad, the Japanese also built a large network of irrigation canals in the Taipei basin, easing greatly the burden of Peihotien's farmers. An irrigation dam built across the river a mile or so upstream from the village lowered the frequency of flooding in the village and ended completely the economic usefulness of the river. Large boats can no longer go freely up and down the stream, and fishing has disintegrated to a sport enjoyed by village boys. The only economic value the river now has for villagers is in the employment of a few of the more destitute women. Building contractors hire them on a piece-work basis to gather stones of a particular size for making concrete. The work is hot, heavy, and miserably paid, but it is vital to several village families during the seasons when the women can find no work weeding fields or cleaning vegetables for market.

Nowadays the river is considered at best a convenient supply of water and at worst a threat, be it real or imagined. Every morning a dozen or so women come down to the river's edge to do their laundry and gossip, and in the evening the village water buffalo are allowed a leisurely soak in the shallow water. For the greater part of the day the beach is deserted. An occasional handful of children venture down to play in the sand, but for most of them the river area is forbidden. During the hot days of summer, busy mothers are hard put to keep their children from wading and by the time they are through primary school, most boys have learned to swim by one stratagem or another. Parental fears are not unjustified. Besides the many drownings that resulted from capsized ferries in the old days, there have been several swimmers lost in more recent years. To the villagers these past drownings add immensely to the realistic dangers of the river since it is believed that the souls of those who drown must remain in the water as unhappy ghosts until they pull in another victim to take their place.

A man in his forties described the ways of ghosts in telling me this bit of local history: "Now I am a person who really doesn't believe in the gods, but sometimes I have to believe. Twenty years ago there used to be a lot more water in the river behind the village than there is now and a lot of people drowned there, but the people who drowned were always people from other places. No one from this village ever drowned in the river except Ong A-cu's husband. This was all because Shang Ti Kung took care of us. When a boat turned over in the river another boat would set out to save the people from the capsized boat. It wasn't that they looked first to see if the people were from this village before they pulled them in, and yet the people from this village always were saved and the people from other places were the ones drowned. The reason Ong A-cu's husband drowned can be easily explained. He was a boatman and you could say that he caused a lot of other people to drown because his boat turned over several times. He broke one of Heaven's laws and so naturally he had to be punished. Besides, if he hadn't died then, the ghosts of the people he had caused to die would be coming back to call him all the time. So, wasn't it better that he drowned himself than to have all those ghosts coming after him all the time?"

The son of another boatman told me of an incident he remembered from his childhood: "Twenty years ago at the end of the eleventh month, the people living here kept hearing someone calling from the other side of the river for the boat to come and get them. This was always at night. But when we went to the river to answer the call, there wouldn't be anyone there. Finally, on the twenty-third day of the twelfth month, my father and I and some workers going to their fields were in the middle of the river when the boat suddenly sank nose first. An old man, a child, and one of the boatmen were drowned. After that, we no longer heard anyone calling at night for the boat. The ghosts had what they wanted."

Peihotien's ghosts are not confined to the river. Several have been seen near a particular bamboo grove, another has repeatedly been seen combing her long hair in the ruins of a pig pen. A quite comfortable room in a house near the village is rarely rented and then only to outsiders because of the unpleasant habits of the ghost of its former owner. According to the druggist in Tapu, ghosts don't really like people and avoid them as much as possible. It is because of this distaste that they are more frequently found in isolated bamboo groves than in busy streets, and in villages rather than in cities

Not all of the people in Peihotien have seen ghosts and certainly not all of them believe in ghosts, but there is not a perfect correlation between a man's belief in ghosts and his level of sophistication in other matters. One of my favorite scoffers in the village is a no-nonsense woman about fifty years old. After listening to some men tell me about the habits of ghosts, she laughed and told me what she thought about ghosts. "I'm always walking around at night and I've never once seen a ghost. When I used to gamble, I wandered around even more at night. I would go all the way to Nanhotien to gamble, come back at midnight for more money, and walk all the way back again. I never met a ghost or even worried about one. Remember where old Ong hung himself on that tree behind their house? Just a few days after his suicide we were gambling at Tan's house. A policeman came and we all had to run and the only way was under that tree. None of us held back. If there was a ghost there, it would been trampled to death we were running so fast. When you are gambling you aren't afraid of the King of Hell. How could you be afraid of a ghost?"

Considering the affinity of ghosts for isolated spots, it seems unlikely that many could stick it out for long in Peihotien. There is very little land within the village that isn't tamed by houses or pig pens or kitchen gardens. Unused land is more or less public property and is crossed and recrossed by dozens of people each day. The square directly behind the house in which we lived is a good example. It is flanked on three sides by houses and on the fourth by the main path through the village. A family who supplements their income by making noodles has set up stretching racks in one corner. Years of use has made the surface of the square as hard and smooth as concrete, ideal for a drying ground. During certain seasons its entire upper half is carpeted with fat rice grains which are turned every few hours for uniform drying. Since the square is public, the families who use it must keep a child stationed there to drive off stray chickens and ducks. Two or three times each summer traveling medicine peddlers set up their make-shift stages in the square, give free performances, and then try to sell their wares to the crowds they attract. Sometimes their acts are elaborated by costumes and a squawking loudspeaker; more often they are simple, lighted by a single electric globe rented from one of the families on the square. During the day a peddler may cycle into the village and spread out his merchandise in the square. The women often do not buy anything and leave the poor peddler to fold his goods back into his box and pedal off to the next village. In the afternoon when the children are home from school, the square is filled with the shrill cries of girls playing a Taiwanese version of hopscotch and boys heatedly debating the success of a shot in a marble game.

At the far end of the village, a distance of only a hundred or so yards, there is another open space even more attractive to the children. Since the houses nearby either have enclosed courtyards or no need for drying grounds, the area is seldom inhibited by adults. It is here that the children come to play the more active games of tag, racing, or, if anyone is fortunate enough to have a ball, a version of soccer. One spring evening when an elaborate tag game was enjoying a period of intense popularity, I counted forty wildly racing children among the sober trees and bushes. In one corner is a guava tree, the fruit of which never ripens because the owner can't keep the children from stealing it while it is green. Shinnying up the tree and trying to grab a hard, green fruit before Mrs. Lim comes yelling out of her house is a favorite adventure with a large group of boys. Near the center of the area is what remains of an old mud and wattling pig pen, the one that is reputed to house a ghost with long hair. The ghost's presence does not discourage the children. The ruins are used as a fort, a castle, an ordinary house, and, more frequently, as a testing ground for skill in climbing and for courage in jumping off. Although the yard has several good-sized trees and many scraggly bushes, it is dominated by a venerable, gnarled tree under which are four or five big boulders. Since I found this spot as inviting as the children on a hot day, I soon learned the many legends attached to the old tree. Because of its extreme age, I was told, it had undoubtedly been a god for many years. A Mrs. Ong, unaware of its high status, had once broken off a limb to chase her ducks. In retaliation the tree-god killed her baby. Another story repeated even more frequently is that the tree houses a huge snake. It is not an ordinary snake but the incarnation of the son of an old man who lives nearby.

As a neighbor told me, "Well, I've never seen the snake myself, but I know lots of people who have. It is really a big one, as big around as your fist. They say it is old Tan's son. He is a man who knows all about gods and bad days and portents, so he ought to know. He saw a little snake under the altar on the night his son was born and then after he got word that his son wouldn't be back from the war, they found this big snake in the tree. Some of the men wanted to kill it because they were afraid it was dangerous, but Old Tan wouldn't let them because he thinks it's his son."

The children have heard this story many times but it no more prevents them from spending long afternoons playing under the tree than the ghost in the pig pen prevents them from hiding there when their mothers are searching for them.

For the children, the women, and a good many of the men, the significant dimensions of the world are the thirty-five or forty brick buildings of Peihotien. With the dramatic increase in population on Taiwan, one corner of a neighboring village now lies just across a paddy field from Peihotien. Yet a woman in search of a moment's chat or a few slices of ginger would rather walk further, within the boundaries of Peihotien, than step across the paddy field to the nearby village. The children of the neighboring villages all go to the same school, but their after-school play groups are composed of village mates—even if they must fill out a team with underaged siblings. A farmer's small plots of land may be scattered among those of farmers from several villages, but in the evening when he is puzzling out a new directory from the Farmer's Association or worrying about the market prices, he does it with the men of Peihotien who may work fields a mile in the opposite direction from his own.

There are several places in the village where groups of adults may be found gossiping or working together at various times of the day. On warm summer evenings the men often fill their rice bowls and retire to the doorstep to eat and chat with a neighbor similarly occupied. A group of families usually share a well and hand pump, and two or three women are there at almost any hour washing out a few clothes not worth carrying all the way to the river, rinsing off a dirty child, or preparing vegetables for the evening meal. The women who live near the irrigation ditch that skirts one edge of the village often gather by the little bridge to clean out a clumsy kettle or rinse out some diapers. A concrete platform on one side of the bridge makes it a popular cooling-off place for children who do not dare go into the river and aren't allowed to play in the precious well water.

For adults the most frequent informal gatherings occur in the three shops of the village. Two of the shops are so small that it takes a practiced eye to identify them. On the square behind the house in which we lived, a family sells cigarettes, matches, a few candies, toilet paper, and similar small items. Here, probably because the family includes some lively teen-agers, is where the older adolescents of the village gather. At the opposite end of the village in a shed that seems in imminent danger of blowing away is a candy store run by a woman with too many children to go out to work and too little money to stay home. The women who come to buy candy to quiet their crying children often sit down on the bench in front of the store to pass the time of day with Mrs. Lim, the proprietress.

The main store and the one most easily identified as a store is located in the center of the village. The candy and cookie collection is more elaborate, and rice, cooking oil, fuel, spices, and a few other essentials can be obtained here at prices only slightly higher than in Tapu. For many years there was no store at all in Peihotien, but according to Ng Kok-hua, the proprietor, our landlord's older brother talked him into fitting out an unused storage wing of his house as a shop. Very little of Mr. Ng's present good fortune comes from the store, but he still keeps it open and probably makes some profit from it. Unfortunately, the bane of a village storekeeper is trying to refuse credit to his neighbors and, when this inevitably fails, trying to collect what he is owed. Occasionally Mr. Ng loses his temper and curses his debtors loudly and publicly. This rarely adds to his income but it does entertain the loungers resting on his benches. One day when Mr. Ng was trying to collect a bad debt from a neighbor who is also a distant relative, I jotted down the highlights of the discussion. Mr. Ng's wife who tends the store most of the time and takes the brunt of her husband's temper was also there. Mr. Ng was saying angrily to his wife, "You think that everyone is of good heart and just give things to them."

Mrs. Ng, looking anxiously at her husband's rising color, answered, "Well, they said they would give me the money after they sold the pig. How could I know that they wouldn't give it to me?"

Mr. Ng gave his wife a look of utter scorn and, turning his attention to the hapless debtor, a Mrs. Lim, he continued, "You all come here and get things and don't give me any money, but when I go buy all these things I have to give money. How can I go along like this? I have to go and borrow money so that I can buy things for the store!"

Some of the on-lookers exchanged skeptical glances over this statement. Mr. Ng did not seem to notice and warmed to his subject. "How can I borrow money and then lend it to other people? That's what it amounts to. And that is no way to do business."

Mrs. Lim answered, soothingly, "Now, Ng, your temper is thin, but my son is not a bad person. It is just that we have no money. The money we got from the pig had to go to people we borrowed money from and we still owe them more money. My poor son is the only one earning money in our family and he has to feed us all. We have to borrow a little each month just to have enough to eat. He only makes NT$700* a month and you can't feed six people on that."

Several of the loungers began at this point to calculate just how much money would be needed to feed a family the size of Mrs. Lim's, and the consensus of opinion was that her son's income was indeed not up to the job. Mr. Ng did not join in these interesting calculations but continued to rub his head and make frustrated comments about the store, debtors, fate, etc. He finally growled at the group in general, "Oh, this store! This store! This store just can't give people food if they don't give it money!"

Mrs. Lim smiled at him sympathetically, and said, "Well, if you had a store in the city, you could do things that way, but not in the country. In the country you have to let people have things whether they have money or not. I know it is hard on you, but you just have to do it that way."

Several members of the group agreed with Mrs. Lim and informed Mr. Ng of it. Mr. Ng began to get red in the face again and spoke very loudly to Mrs. Lim. "You calculate how much interest it would cost you if you borrowed two thousand dollars a year. You just see how much interest that would be every month. Now, I don't charge you a single bit of interest, do I? Do I?"

Mrs. Lim looked genuinely horrified at the thought and readily agreed that he did not charge interest. Mr. Ng continued, "So now all I want is my money. You just give me the money and not the interest— just the money so that I can go buy more things for my store. When you go home, you tell that son of yours to bring me my money and I will be happy. I don't care if you never buy anything from me again, but I want my money. I won't say anything about that stupid nephew of yours who has three people in the family that are working and still comes and buys on credit and never pays me back."

* At this time the exchange rate for New Taiwan dollars (NT$) was about forty to one United States dollar. For a village family of two adults and two children approximately NT$800 would provide an average living, with very few luxuries.

This seemed to lead Mr. Ng to think of all the others who had debts with him and he listed them and their debts and their incomes and their ancestors, all in an unsavory light. He ended with a dramatic wail, "Everyone wants to eat me—who am I supposed to eat?" and disappeared into the back of the store. Before the crowd had a chance to move off though, he called out to his wife in a fine stage voice, "Old woman! From now on don't you give anything to anybody without seeing their money."

The women sitting on the benches chatted for a while longer and even though some of them were on Mr. Ng's list, they were generally sympathetic to the plight of the country storekeeper. One woman summed it up nicely: "It really is hard to run a country store if you don't have a lot of money because all of your neighbors that you have known for generations and all of your relatives come and want things when they don't have any money, and so you just have to give them the things. Sometimes you know that if you give things to this person, he will never give you the money, and so you tell him this, and then he gets mad and says that you don't respect him and goes all around to people saying you have insulted his family. If you don't give things to people, they get mad at you, but if you do, you can't make any money. It really is hard to run a store in the country."

chapter 3

HOUSES
AND
FAMILIES

The interaction of the Taiwanese villager with his friends and neighbors is like the spice in his soup, savory but of little sustenance. It is with
his family, his parents and grandparents, his children and grandchildren,
that he takes the measure of his life. His relations with his parents
may be strained, with his wife distant, and with his children formal,
but without these people he would be an object of pity and of no small
amount of suspicion. He would be pitied because he had no parents to
"help" him and no children to support him in his old age, pitied
because he had no place in a group, because he didn't belong any-
where. For these same reasons he would be the object of suspicion. A
man not thoroughly imbedded in a network of kinship cannot be
completely trusted because he cannot be dealt with in the normal way.
If he behaves improperly, one cannot discuss his behavior with his
brother or seek redress from his parents. If one wants to approach
him about a delicate matter, one cannot use his uncle as a go-between
to prepare the way. Wealth cannot make up for this deficiency any
more than it can make up for the loss of arms and legs. Money has no
past, no future, and no obligations. Relatives do. A young man
orphaned as an adolescent or otherwise separated from his immediate
kinsmen commonly marries into his wife's family. As this usually
involves his agreeing to assign some of his children to his wife's
father's line of descent, a man who marries in this fashion bears the
stigma of having abandoned his parents and his ancestors—but this is
preferable to an isolated existence. A man with a good job could find
a wife among the entertainers of the city, but he wants more than a

wife. He wants the security of a stable and permanent network of human relations.

The farm houses of Taiwan are symbolic of this attitude toward the family. In Taipei and in the larger market towns there have always been houses designed for rental income, houses for transients who may stay a month or ten years, but they are barren houses designed only for the present occupants and not looking toward the future. In the country, even today, when a man builds a house he follows the old pattern. He builds with a vision of housing under one roof a large and prosperous family of many generations. Farmers are rarely wealthy on Taiwan. Although they are just as likely as anyone else to try to implement their dreams, they do so with a shrewd practicality. Instead of hoarding gold or borrowing money to build the huge U-shaped structure that is to house generations as yet unborn, they build the base of their future, a strong rectangular building. At each end of the rectangle, however, there are indications of the ultimate design—an unnecessary door, a carefully made archway clumsily boarded over until the day it will open into a new wing housing the family of a son or a grandson. The rectangle becomes first an L and finally a U whose arms may be extended again and again.

That part of Peihotien that lies upstream is often referred to as "Brick House Place," a designation that has survived from the building of the first all-brick house. Before that, houses were built of mud over bamboo wattling and roofed with rice thatch. A family who could tear down one of their mud walls and replace it with strong red bricks showed a sign of prosperity; their continuing good fortune could be seen in the replacement of another wall a few years later. Now only unimportant buildings like pig pens or storage rooms have mud walls and all of the thatch has been replaced with shining tile roofs. There are mud houses left in the other villages of Hotien, but Peihotien exhibits its superiority in a rich display of red brick. Nowadays a new house begins in brick and tile.

The first step a family takes toward building a new house is to summon a geomancer. He is shown the family land and is expected to site the house in the position most favorable to the natural and supernatural phenomena. Evidently these variables are fairly uniform in a small area for nearly all of the houses of Peihotien face in the same direction, away from the river—sad from the point of view of Western aesthetics but undoubtedly well justified in terms of geomancy. Before any construction begins, the family and the geomancer make careful enquiries of priests, the elderly, even the gods, to be sure that the house is not placed on the site of an old temple or shrine. Indignant gods could bring untold misery on the family for generations. When construction is underway, the geomancer supervises the building of the ritually important cooking stove, a large, square, brick structure which is intimately tied to the welfare of the family. If it is clumsily built, or improperly oriented, misfortune or even death may come to family members. The family must also prevent those who bear them ill will from secretly inserting dangerous magical objects in the partially constructed stove. If the carpenters and bricklayers are ill-paid or disrespectfully treated, they too might practice various forms of witchcraft on the stove or on the main roof beam. The welfare of the family in both the present and the future generations is irrevocably involved in the construction of their home.

The original rectangle of a new rural home may vary somewhat in size, floor plan, or interior decoration, but the basic outline is the same for all. In the center of the front wall of each house are double doors which open into the guest hall. In most houses the floor of the guest hall is of beaten earth, the same as the other rooms of the house, but in more affluent homes the hall is distinguished by a concrete floor. The one village home with concrete floors throughout displays a terrazzo floor in the guest hall. This room is the stage on which a family presents itself to the world. Here one often finds a scroll of unexpected quality and such luxuries as a radio or a sewing machine; here also are the material representations of the family's charter, their ancestral tablets. These are flat, rectangular slips of wood, rounded on the top like grave stones, each inscribed in black ink with the posthumous name of a deceased member of the family. In every home these are arranged on a tall, narrow altar table set against the wall opposite the front door. To the foreign eye this altar is a clutter of religious paraphernalia, but there is order here if not neatness. The gods take precedence over the ancestors and their images are thus always to the right of the altar; men take precedence over women and thus the tablets of men are always to the right of those of their wives. Where the tablets are arranged in a small lacquer box, the more recently deceased are at the front of the box; where they are arranged on open shelves, the most distant ancestors stand on the top of the shelf at the head of a pyramid.

Individually, the tables have little significance. They are simply a focal point for burning offerings in honor of the parent who was respected if not loved. Collectively, however, they are the symbol of something larger. They are proof of an unbroken chain of men beginning in a distant past of splendid achievements, a past in which the insignificant farmer burning incense was represented by his own blood relatives even though not himself present. Through him and because of him the chain will pass to his sons and his son's sons into an equally splendid world of the future in which he will again be represented though not present. For many Taiwanese, both the humble who accept their religion without question and the sophisticated who scoff at its mysticism, it is this concept of being one link in an awesomely long chain, unimportant in themselves yet essential to the continuation of the chain, that gives meaning to what might be an unkind world of hard work and hunger. Every new bride brings hope of at least one more link in the chain of descent; every birth brings certainty. Both bride and infant are formally introduced to the ancestors shortly after their entrance into the family. At every death the ancestors are respectfully notified that another family member is passing over to their side of the altar.

Although the guest hall is also the ancestral hall, the scene of all the ceremonies connected with them as well as many involving the hierarchy of the gods, the room is not a sacred one. The altar is high enough to be safe from the hands of toddlers and awesome enough to be safe from their older siblings, but its very height provides underneath an excellent play house, train station, or opera stage for children on rainy afternoons. In the cold, damp days of winter, the guest hall is nearly always busy with the games of active youngsters. This is also the room in which tables are set up for the banquets that occur regularly throughout the year in rural Taiwan. The head of a household with business interests meets his customers here at his desk against one wall. When he is not home, the children use the desk to do their homework. When a typhoon threatens, the farmer comes in every few hours to listen to the weather report, leaning casually against the altar. In the hot, humid days of summer, he may take a short nap here after the noon meal, stretched out on the cool cement floor. The guest hall is kept somewhat cleaner than the other rooms in the house and is more frequently seen by strangers than the other rooms, but it is not sacred.

Leading from both sides of the guest hall are hallways along which the bedrooms are located. Reflecting the principles of seniority found in the ancestral tablets, the members of the family are assigned sleeping rooms according to their status in the family. The head of the family takes the rooms to the right of the ancestors; his younger brother or married sons, the rooms to the left. An old grandmother usually shares a bed with her grandchildren, enjoying with the warmth of their young bodies the satisfaction that she has by her own efforts produced at least two more generations for the family. Some sleeping rooms in Peihotien are furnished with the traditional carved and can-nopied wooden beds, massive and often ugly; others contain only Japanese *tatami* sleeping platforms. The platforms have many advan-tages, particularly for families with numerous children, since their capacity is practically unlimited. They are also considerably cooler during the stifling summer nights when the old-fashioned, box-like beds become as hot as ovens.

The kitchen is usually located at one end of the rectangle, al-though some families house it in a shed at the back of the basic structure. Wherever it is, the central feature of the room is the large, square brick stove. Few families have the luxury of a room set aside for dining and are content to take their meals in one corner of the kitchen. If the room is too small, or if the family tends toward elegant living, they eat in the guest hall. Family meals are considerably less formal than Western meals. If the night is hot, a man fills his bowl with rice, tops it with whatever relish or vegetable his wife has pro-vided, and then squats in the cool breeze of the doorway. His wife seldom sits at the table, eating her rice as best she can while supervis-ing the children and watching the soup. The older children may follow their father's example and wander off into the yard, skillfully manag-ing the rice bowl and chopsticks while watching a game of hopscotch. In large families this is the only way the meals can be managed, since it would be impossible for them all to sit down at once. The Chinese custom of feeding the men first is acknowledged but difficult to prac-tice when the men's hours are determined by different occupations. More commonly the food is simply put on the table and whoever is there eats—at the table, if he likes, or on the back stoop, if he prefers.

When a man builds a house, his fondest dream is that within his lifetime one or even both of the wings will be added to the original rectangle to house his sons and married grandsons. In the ideal Taiwanese family several generations of fathers and sons live with

their wives under the same roof, sharing, under the supervision of the
eldest male of the eldest generation, their labor and their wealth. This
ideal is occasionally achieved by the wealthy, but among the poor,
two married brothers rarely maintain a joint household after the death
of their father. The wife of one is too sure that the wife of the other
feeds her children more when it is her turn to cook, or that she shirks
her share of the housework. While the brothers' mother is still living
and active, she can control or at least mediate disputes in the kitchen,
but the loser of any dispute is sure to whisper to her husband about
the favoritism his parents are showing to the other brother's children.
The relationship between brothers is often not sturdy enough to withstand the constant harrassment of their wives. As boys, the elder was
required to yield to the younger in all things. If they quarreled, their
parents punished the elder, regardless of who was in the right, since he
was supposed "to know better." Yet as adults, their roles are re-
versed. The elder brother makes the decisions and the younger is
expected to acquiesce. As often as not, the younger brother, quite
unused to submission, finds this situation unbearable. As long as their
father is alive, the decisions about managing the family property may
be issued in his name, coating the younger brother's pill and delaying
an open rupture. Often this is not enough and shortly after the
younger's marriage, the brothers divide the family property, from then
on retaining their earnings for the use of their own small families.

In most cases the two families created by the division remain
under the same roof, but a strategic door is nailed shut to separate the
two apartments, or a bamboo fence appears across the courtyard.
They continue to use the guest hall equally, but its neatness and
elegance decline noticeably if there is not a mother-in-law present to
bully the young wives into greater attention. The most dramatic
change occurs in the kitchen. If the guest hall can be considered the
symbol of the larger family, the stove is the symbol of the living
family. Members of a family are defined as those who share a cooking
stove; the colloquial term for the act of family division is literally "the
dividing of the stove." This identification of stove and family is so
important that those who cannot afford to add a room to house the
stove of a newly created family unit build a second stove in the same
kitchen.

Over half of the houses in Peihotien have one of the intended
wings and some have both. For all but two families, only the external

structure of their ideal is complete. Instead of housing a single, united family, the wings are filled with independent units, each with its own stove, each having broken from the main family at the time of a brother's marriage or a father's death. Instead of a large house, the structure can only be properly described as a compound, for in some of the older houses the families are related to each other only three or four generations back. Two families have kept the ideal after the death of their fathers. One is a pair of surprisingly amiable brothers, both of whom work out of the village at well-paid jobs, leaving their two wives, ten children, unmarried sister, and mother in an ample village home. The two wives are so alike they could be sisters and they work together in effortless cooperation. Before we left the village, however, one of the brothers had been transferred to a town too far away to return home more than once a week. His wife, knowing only too well how much business is contracted in what might be called Taiwanese night clubs, packed up her children and the furniture of her dowry and went to join him. Although the division was made with little fuss and continued good will, it was still recognized as a "dividing of the stove." The only family still retaining the eminence of being united under one authority when we left Peihotien was that of Lim Chieng-cua. This is the family with whom we lived and about whom the rest of this book is concerned.

Lim Chieng-cua and his siblings were born and grew up in a small mud house much like their neighbors. In time a good many improvements were made in the house, but the family really wanted a new one, not additions and improvements. Lim Chieng-cua once told me, "Before we built this new house, we had a mud house with a thatch roof. Every time there was a typhoon my father and my older brother's wife and I had to stay up all night to tie the roof down so it wouldn't blow off. Oh, how badly we wanted a new house! We changed two rooms of the mud house to brick, we had a good kitchen, a room for bathing and a big wooden tub for heating bath water. We even had a hand pump and hardly anyone had a pump in those days, but our hearts weren't satisfied. Now we have a good brick house, and yet every time I see a better house, I wish we had a better one too."

It is characteristic of Lim Chieng-cua and his father that when they built their new house it was not quite like any other house in the village. It was a traditional house and in every way worthy of respect,

but it was undeniably different. At that time the family was not particularly large: Lim Chieng-cua was not yet married and his elder
brother wasn't living at home. Speculative neighbors might have expected the Lims to build the usual bottom wing of the U, adding a
new wing, if their prosperity continued, when Lim Chieng-cua married. Instead, the Lims built a truly large house, a house that is still
the largest in Peihotien. Due to the unusual individuality that has
given the Lims a reputation for wisdom and leadership—a habit of
seeing as important the same things as their neighbors but not feeling
required to follow the conventional paths to their goals—Lim Chieng-
cua and his father departed slightly from the usual practice. Rather
than building a U-shaped house, they built their house in the form of
a hollow square, leaving a small open courtyard in the center. The
front of the square, however, deviated in no way from the conventional base for a U-shaped structure, even to the doorways for expan-
sion at each end. They surrounded the house and the drying ground in
front with a dignified brick wall, a useful addition in the city, but one
rarely found in the northern villages now that bandit attacks are no
longer feared. They also built a long, handsome brick pig pen, a final
touch which both amused and awed their neighbors.

The Lims' guest hall is quite a large room, as it would have to be
to retain proper proportions with the rest of the house. It is floored
with lovely terrazzo, neatly and soberly. The floor is swept more often
than in the other rooms and mopped every week or so. Puddles left by
diaperless children are cleaned up fairly quickly, and concerted effort
keeps the chickens and ducks from seeking shelter there. When we
first moved into the house, there was no ceiling in the guest hall. The
whitewashed walls stretched up to heavy beams richly darkened by
years of incense smoke. Unfortunately, in his restless desire to improve and change, Lim Chieng-cua added a ceiling to the room. His
neighbors consider it attractive, but I missed the stark dignity of those
beams.

The Lims' guest hall is simply furnished, far more simply than
their income requires. The prosperous families of Peihotien buy
heavy, overstuffed chairs covered in plastic. In summer they are a
torment to sit on for more than a few minutes, and in winter they
smell musty and develop miniature landscapes of mold. The Lims,
whether from modesty or from a more developed sense of comfort,
retain the old rattan chairs that are comfortable year around. The
family altar is another matter. Modesty here would not be a virtue: a

man is expected to provide his ancestors with the best he can possibly manage. The Lim altar is tastefully simple, but of excellent wood and careful carving. The top is cluttered with the usual collection of ugly vases, gaudy lanterns, fussy brass candle holders, an elaborately carved wooden stand to hold the half-moon-shaped divining blocks, and some delicate pewter wine cups used only to offer drink to the gods and ancestors. Besides the ancestral tablets, the altar also holds two glass boxes containing images of the Goddess of Mercy and Tu Ti Kung. The latter are only decoration. Although they have vague protective powers, they are not imbued with the significance of the images residing in temples. On the wall behind the altar are a picture of the Eight Immortals and a large panel covered with the character for long life repeated in its hundred different forms. The only other decorations in the room are a Chinese painting on a scroll and various inscriptions painted or pasted over doors and windows to insure the family's good health, prosperity, and fertility.

When my husband and I moved into the Lim family home, we were delighted to be given as our sleeping room the tiny room directly in back of the family altar. The room is separated from the guest hall by only half a wall topped by a lattice screen. There was little chance of our sleeping through any of the religious ceremonies performed at dawn or during the night. Much to my surprise, the sleeping room that should have housed the head of the family became our office. It had been empty since the death of Lim Chieng-cua's father. Later, when I came to understand the structure and tensions of the family, I was impressed by Lim Chieng-cua's discretion, and the diplomacy with which he had solved a vexing problem. At the time, I was simply pleased at the ease with which we had inserted ourselves into the very center of a Taiwanese family. We had little peace and quiet, and no privacy, but for our purposes the situation was ideal.

The remainder of the Lim's front wing is taken up with sleeping rooms—Lim Chieng-cua and his wife and six children on one side, his elder brother's widow, Lim A-pou, her married son and his family on the other. At one end, in a room that would have been the kitchen in a smaller house, is the dining room, one of the few in the village. Its elegance is confined to its title. Though fairly large, the room is cluttered with crocks of pickled vegetables, the big rice bin, a foot-treadle sewing machine, and odds and ends of farm equipment. In the center of the room is a high, round eating table with an assortment of tall stools around it. The stools are drawn from those stacked in the corner with a dozen or more table tops, stored there until needed in the guest hall for big feasts. Off the dining room, in the side wing of the house, is another sleeping room. This room is occupied most of the time by Lim A-pou's unmarried son, but he usually has to share the *tatami* sleeping platform with visiting children, male relatives, and whatever hired hands happen to be living in the house. Beyond this room is the busiest room in the house, the kitchen. Except on the coldest or stormiest days, the door between the kitchen and the small internal courtyard is kept open for light and ventilation. Most of the floor space is taken up by the huge brick cooking stove which boasts two, rather than the usual single, shallow cooking pans. One corner is filled with a heap of long paper strips, residue from Lim Chieng-cua's cement bag factory. The paper is twisted into hanks and fed into the stove by the women as they cook, by children when they can be caught, and, on cold days, by the men, if they have time to lounge before the evening meal. The walls are dark and dirty with accumula-tions of smoke and grease. Baskets, rice cake molds, tea kettles, and various other cooking utensils hang at random from pegs. Two closed cupboards hold dishes, rice bowls, cups, chopsticks, and bits of food that need protection from the animals that wander into the house. The kitchen has a convenience that is the envy of every woman in the village and that was a source of considerable misgiving to me. The well and the open cistern into which the water is pumped are located in the kitchen itself. My uneasiness arose from the fact that the next room contained, besides another small stove for the preparation of pig food, the Japanese style toilet. What we euphemistically refer to as "night-soil" is stored until needed for the fields, or until the pit is full, not ten feet from the water supply.

I was never sure just how the wing across the back of the house had been used formerly, but it may have been the original location of the cement bag factory. When we arrived, part of it was used for storage and part of it was taken up with the small bathing room. The storage room was cleared for us to use as a dining room and a sleeping room for our cook and our interpreter. Our long-suffering cook acquisitioned an alcove in the hallway to the bathing room for her coal oil stove. The rest of the back wing was occupied by another family of renters during the first part of our stay, but when they left we took over this space to house our expanding staff and to provide ourselves with a much needed testing room.

Lim Chieng-cua's restlessness was expressed in several changes in the house during our stay. The first was the ceiling in the guest hall. It was followed by a gigantic electric ceiling fan which had the effect of a stationary tornado the few times it was turned on. I think the next change was the one appreciated equally by our citified cook and the women of the Lim family, all of whom hated the clumsy hand pump that was once so admired by their neighbors. The operation began with the installation of an electric pump to fill the cistern, but continued until Lim Chieng-cua had built a tank on the roof for pressure and threaded ugly, constantly clogging pipes into the family kitchen, our kitchen alcove, and the bathing room. When the system worked it was a joy, but Lim Chieng-cua soon discovered some of the handicaps of Western "conveniences." At least once a month he could be found pulling his pump apart or poking at the clogged waterpipes. This gave his neighbors small satisfaction. The last improvement— one that motivated one of the villagers to suggest that we must be paying far more rent than either we or the Lims were willing to admit—was the introduction of a Western bathtub. Until this monstrosity arrived, the bathing room had been occupied by a handsome wooden tub under which a small fire was built each evening. The water was never hot but always warm enough to be comfortable. Its operations left nothing to be desired. One stood on the brick floor and laddled water onto one's back as slowly or as rapidly as desired. The water drained across the floor into one of the gutters that ran through all of the back rooms and that was the end of it. One day the wooden tub was yanked out and in its place appeared a lizard green, pressed-stone, full length bathtub. A hole was poked in the wall and on the other side was placed what Americans would consider an antique water heater, a round drum with space at the bottom for a small coal fire. After what I hope was an appropriately polite period of using the new bath tub, i.e., scrubbing it out, waiting half an hour for it to slowly fill, bathing, waiting ten minutes for it to empty, scrubbing it out, etc., I returned to my practice of ladling water over myself on the brick floor. Not so the rest of the family, nor, for that matter, the rest of the village. Lim Chieng-cua's latest addition became a treat among his friends, and on nights when the women of the family were feeling lavish with fuel, innumerable shining faces made the journey through our kitchen to the green bathtub.

There are fourteen permanent members of the Lim household.

The police registration for the house lists Lim Chieng-cua and his wife, Lim Chui-ieng; their six children; Lim Chieng-cua's older brother's widow, Lim A-pou; her unmarried son, Masa; her married son, Lim A-bok, and his wife; and their two children. During the two years we lived with them, the Lim family always had at least one other relative accepting their hospitality. The enormous task of providing for this large family is shared by the adult members of the household according to a careful division of labor. As the eldest male, and therefore the head of the family, Lim Chieng-cua serves as general manager, deciding when and how the family income is to be used, and, being the most worldly member of the family, he also manages the family business, the cement bag factory that employs from four to twelve village girls. Lim A-bok, a man in his late twenties, takes primary responsibility for farming the family's five or six acres of land, arranging for the sale of its produce as well. In the kitchen, Lim A-pou's daughter-in-law and Lim Chieng-cua's wife share the large task of cooking for the family, each woman taking the responsibility for five days at a time. In so far as he does anything, Masa helps his older brother in the fields. Lim A-pou's main responsibility is gathering, chopping, and cooking food for the family's dozen or so pigs, but with her amazing energy and efficiency, she also finds time to help her slow daughter-in-law in the kitchen, and during the rush seasons of harvest and planting, she works with her sons in the fields.

This division of labor enables the family to support itself much more efficiently than if they were divided into smaller nuclear family units. As he is physically unable to do heavy labor himself, Lim Chieng-cua needs someone to farm his share of the family land, and for his part, Lim A-bok has neither the experience nor possibly the temperament to run the family business. Although an intelligent man, he has not yet developed his uncle's easy and effective manner of expressing himself, nor has he the reputation as a leader in the community that this skill has brought Lim Chieng-cua. Because of Lim A-bok's skill and industry as a farmer, however, he occupies an unusual position in the community for a man his age. The farmers of the village, old and young alike, choose him to represent them in the various government and cooperative farm groups and look to him for the interpretation and evaluation of the information received from these groups. For the women of the family, the arrangement has the advantage of giving each of them a break from the monotony of kitchen duties as well as comparatively long periods of time they can devote to sewing, the care of their children, or even visits to their natal families.

A visitor to the home might conclude that these arrangements function quite smoothly. The family's meals are always well cooked and served at regular times; the children are usually as neat or neater than the neighbors' children; the house is kept reasonably clean and in good repair; the family's land is always cultivated and the general appearance of the fields is neat and orderly; the factory seems busy most of the time. In short, the various members of the family perform their particular duties efficiently and effectively. To see the less fortunate effects, one has to look beneath the surface of the family's daily routines. As Lim Chui-ieng once told me, "If you look at the face of our family, it looks good, but if you look at its bones, it's not like that." In the "bones" of the family there is ceaseless friction between the two major units: Lim Chieng-cua's family and Lim A-pou's family. For the most part their conflict is wordless, expressed only by the emotional distance between them, but on occasion the tempers flare, revealing the true intensity of the tensions below. To understand the conflicts that existed within these people as well as those that existed between them, it is necessary to look at some of the events of their childhood. To understand why they have resisted for so long the pressures that divided every other family in Peihotien, it is necessary to look at the domestic climate in which they grew up.

chapter 4

LIM HAN-CI: THE FATHER

The desire to simplify the character of the dead, to be done with the variations of mood that complicate day to day interactions, to indulge in the luxury of absolutes, seems to be a universal human tendency. The father of the present head of the Lim family has been dead for less than a decade, but already the story-tellers of Peihotien have woven the many anecdotes about him into the uncertain fabric of legend. Lim Han-ci's dour personality, his tremendous strength, his harshness, the determination with which he worked—all have become part of the legend. Even when the saga is modified by reminiscences of those who knew him as father, grandfather, or trusted friend, there emerges a personality from which epics are born. He was a hard man. He spoke little and then only after putting considerable thought into his choice of words. His temper terrified his family and neighbors, and he used it more as a technique he summoned at will than a fault he could not control. His justice was as harsh as his voice. Although liberties may have been taken with Lim Han-ci's character since his death, the fact remains that he has had no small effect on his children and on his community.

If Lim Han-ci had any brothers, they died before marriage. A married brother would have left descendants in the village, and there were none. Whether or not Lim Han-ci had sisters is difficult to say. I was never introduced to a sister or a sister's child, but this does not mean they do not exist. Women marry out of their natal village and often their children lose all contact with their mother's relatives. All I could learn of Lim Han-ci's childhood is that his father earned a precarious living as a tenant farmer and that Lim Han-ci spent a large part of his adult life working the same land as a tenant. Even as a young man he had a reputation as a tireless worker, and when he married and began having children, anecdotes about his unceasing labor multiplied. One of his former neighbors told me that even during the New Year celebrations when everyone else in the village was gambling or visiting friends, Lim Han-ci was weeding his sweet potatoes. Several people insist that this is how he got his personal name, Han-ci or Sweet Potato, but this is doubtful. Parents commonly give their sons deprecatory nicknames such as Small Snake, or Thin Dog, hoping by this display of scorn to make their most valued possession less attractive to malicious ghosts. In Lim Han-ci's day, sweet potatoes were the food of the poor.

Whether or not Lim Han-ci's sweet potatoes are relevant to his personal name, his reputation for hard work was second to none. His son, Lim Chieng-cua, verified this: "My father was a man who worked hard for his family. He didn't smoke and he didn't drink, and he could do two and a half times more work in a day than an ordinary man. Sometimes during the planting season he slept only two or three hours a night. Even as an old man he wouldn't rest, and when we begged him to rest he would say, 'When I cannot work, I will die.' "

Every tenant farmer on Taiwan works hard just to earn enough food for his family, and he who works harder than others is not necessarily going to benefit more. In Lim Han-ci's youth, tenant farmers had little chance of saving money and still less of saving enough to buy their own land. The most they could hope for was that their sons or their sons' sons would get an education or a start in a small business. Lim Han-ci, however, combined with his energy a stubborn intelligence and a fierce pride. In one way or another he saved enough money to buy several small pieces of land. The few catties of rice that were now his instead of the landlord's did not appreciably alter Han-ci's own standard of living, and yet they represented an enormous achievement. He had done something few of his neighbors could accomplish, and he had made a permanent contribution to the welfare of his family. A peasant farmer does not think in terms of his own welfare and that of his immediate family; he calculates his accomplishments in terms of their benefits to all of his descendants. Lim Han-ci's little land would not produce many catties of rice in his own lifetime, but it would help support his children, his grandchildren, and his descendants for generations to come. With this beginning the family's land would increase—their harvests would buy more land, the family would prosper and grow. In this Lim Han-ci could take great satisfaction. As a well-known proverb puts it, "Succeeding is like a turtle climbing up a mountain." Lim Han-ci had taken the first few steps up that mountain, and with the vision of the long climb ahead he disciplined himself and his family. He was well aware of the other half of the proverb: "Failing is like water running down a hill."

Lim Han-ci was respected and grudgingly admired, but his Puritan temperament did not endear him to his contemporaries. He knew all there was to know about farming and when he decided on an innovation in the customary way of doing things, his neighbors usually followed him. He was not an active member of the groups of men who sat around on summer evenings, talking and smoking, but when an important decision had to be made, he was always consulted. He was not a man to ignore or to take advantage of. An old farmer of his own generation told me, "He would help anyone who asked for help, but he treated very unceremoniously and very severely anyone who tried to put something over on him. He often gave water from his rice paddies to those who asked him for it, but he would starve a man before he gave him the water if he tried to steal it in the night. He was a man who would 'eat the soft, but not the hard.'" And, if the adults walked quietly around Lim Han-ci, children literally fled at the sight of him. Aside from his known disapproval of any form of play or frivolity, he was also renowned for his fiery temper. Even his own children admit to being terrified of him.

In the shadow of such a glowering personage it is not surprising that little is remembered about Lim Han-ci's wife. Her adopted daughters and her grandchildren describe her as a quiet woman of gentle kindness who worked hard but always had time for a frightened or hurt child. No one in the village mentions her, and the family rarely talks about her except on the anniversary of her death when they argue over what might have been her favorite food so that they can send it to her in offerings. She must have died before the marriage of her second son because Lim Chui-ieng, who complains about everything else, does not complain about her mother-in-law. Her children speak of her with warmth and fondness, but she is now only a memory. Perhaps they remember her gentleness and think of her in quiet moments, but it is their father whose example continues to guide their lives. Their mother was only a woman and died; their father created for the family a reputation and standards that survive in his name. He became a symbol of what the family could and should be, and as a symbol he is still present—as much a reality as he was when alive.

Lim Han-ci's wife was a fortunate woman in one respect. The first child she bore her husband was a son, Lim Hue-lieng. A bride comes to her new home as a complete stranger, both to the family and to her husband. For the first year or two she has the duties of, and little more status than, a servant. She is expected to release her mother-in-law from the drudgery of cleaning and cooking, bring her morning tea, help her dress, and see to her comfort in every way. In the days of Lim Han-ci, a bride also had the humiliating task of washing her mother-in-law's foot bindings and rewrapping the twisted, deformed feet. She was expected to serve her father-in-law's meals whenever he wished them, with her eyes lowered and her mouth shut. Unless summoned to fill his pipe or perform some other service, she avoided his presence. To her husband, a man whom she had not met until the day of her marriage, she was also subservient. If ill temper prompted him to beat her, she must accept it without complaint. She was expected to provide his meals, keep his clothes in order, and, in the old days, make his and the rest of the family's cloth shoes. Above all, she was expected to provide the family with a son—the means of continuing their line of descent. The life of a bride today is considerably less onerous, but there has been no change in the family's primary requirement of her. Until she produces a son, she has no secure place in the family. Bearing a girl at least gives evidence of her ability to bear children; the birth of a son ends the anxiety in her husband's family and gives her at last an undeniable status in it.

Probably Lim Han-ci's next child was a girl, but for this I must rely on hearsay and my knowledge of other village families. During our first weeks in the village, Lim Chieng-cua spent nearly as much time interviewing us as we did interviewing him. As a result he had a fair knowledge of what Chinese practices were not common in the United States and a cunning instinct for the kinds of things we were not to be told about his own family. He was extremely cooperative in explaining the idiosyncracies of other family genealogies and the disposition of their unwanted children, but in theory the gods had not blessed his family with any unwanted children. His neighbors, however, were equally cooperative in discussing the Lim family genealogy. By their account, after the birth of Lim Hue-lieng, his mother bore a girl. To Lim Han-ci as well as to his neighbors, raising a girl is a luxury.

As soon as a daughter is old enough to be useful in the house or in the fields, she is also old enough to marry and leave the family (at no small expense to her parents) to give her labor and her sons to another family. The general village attitude is summed up in the words of an old lady who told me why she disposed of her daughters: "Why should I want so many daughters? It is useless to raise your own daughters. I'd just have to give them away when they were grown, so when someone asked for them as infants I gave them away. Think of all the rice I saved."

Faced with a luxury in which he did not want to indulge, Lim Han-ci took the same course. The girl was given to another family as a "little bride," to be raised as a wife for one of their sons. As Lim Han-ci's wife had milk to nurse a child, the family then adopted a girl from a third family to raise as a wife for their own son, Lim Hue-lieng. The family thus ridded themselves of a "useless" daughter and acquired a girl, Lim A-pou, who could marry their son and perpetuate their line of descent. In giving away their own daughter they saved themselves the expense of raising her and providing her dowry; in adopting another child in her place they avoided paying an extrava-gant bride price for an adult daughter-in-law. Marriages involving a "little bride" do not have the prestige of those that bring a daughter-in-law into the home as a young adult, but they are recognized by local custom throughout northern Taiwan and were common among poor peasant families at the time. Nearly half of the village men of Lim Han-ci's generation married in this fashion. The early and prolonged association of husband and wife often affects their later marital rela-tionship, but this is not considered adequate reason for foregoing the advantages of such a marriage. The desires of the parents and the needs of the family take precedence over the personal interest of the children.

In the ten years between the birth of Lim Hue-lieng and Lim Chieng-cua several unexpected things happened to Lim Han-ci's fam-ily. A year or two after the adoption of Lim A-pou another son was born. For one reason or another, probably simply because a suitable child became available, Tan A-hong was adopted at once to be his future wife. Unfortunately, this second son died before the age of two from one of the many diseases that afflict Chinese infants. To make matters worse, when Tan A-hong was nine or ten, the girl the family had given away to make room for Lim A-pou was returned to them because the boy she was to marry in her foster family had also died. This placed Lim Han-ci in an awkward position, one that endangered the shaky balance a tenant farmer maintains with his poverty. Lim A-pou, the girl adopted to marry their eldest son, was old enough to be useful around the house and was proving to be a hard worker. Tan A-hong, adopted to marry the son who died, was still too young to work in the fields and was not particularly needed around the house. When their natural daughter was returned to them, Lim Han-ci found himself with two "useless" girls to feed, clothe, and marry to other families. He solved the problem of Tan A-hong by reselling her to another family; he accepted his fate by keeping his natural daughter. In view of the subsequent histories of the two girls, the decision was probably a wise one, but it must have been difficult at the time. Lim Han-ci's daughter grew up in her own family, made a good marriage, and returned to the house during my stay only on appropriate ceremonial occasions. Her siblings and foster siblings are fond of her, and she and her husband make no more than the usual demands on the family. Tan A-hong's relationship with the family should have ended at the point she left them, but they were plagued by her problems for years to come. She finally returned to settle permanently in Peihotien about half way through my stay in the village.

Lim Chieng-cua was the next son born to Lim Han-ci and although never very strong, he survived the dangers of a Chinese childhood. Two years later another daughter was born to the family, but she lived for little more than a month. To soothe the maternal sorrow and to provide Lim Chieng-cua with a wife, Iu Mui-mue was adopted almost immediately.

The last child born to Lim Han-ci's wife was also a girl. She was given away as soon as she was weaned and to my knowledge never returns to visit the family, not even on the traditional homecoming festival of the New Year. This is not unusual behavior on the part of children given away in adoption. Proverbially—and from my observation there is a great deal of truth in the proverbs—adopted daughters are treated harshly by their foster parents. Not all female adoptions are to provide sons with wives. Some little girls are adopted simply as daughters, similar to the Western form of adoption; others are adopted, usually by the wealthy, for their labor. Sometimes the small slave girls fall into the hands of frustrated women who vent on them the aggression they dare not express toward their husbands and parents-in-law. Even the girls adopted to be wives of the family's sons are never accorded the treatment of daughters born into the family. One of the most effective threats mothers make to recalcitrant children is to threaten them with adoption. In describing a sobbing, woebegone child, people often say, "Oh, there she is, crying like an adopted daughter." One might expect a fair number of adopted daughters to hate their foster parents and to regard the holidays requiring a visit to their natal homes as oases in the desert of their everyday existence. This is not the case at all. Their resentment is directed at the natal parents who sent them into this hard life, and they cling with something akin to panic to the foster parents who treat them so coldly. This is not the place to go into the psychological implications of these attitudes but that they exist was brought home to me again and again in interviews with adopted daughters, their bewildered parents, and their foster parents.

Lim Han-ci comes closer to the Western stereotype of the Chinese patriarch than do the heads of most Taiwanese families. Most fathers in Peihotien administer an occasional lecture or a formal beating, but the mothers do most of the disciplining, teaching, and directing of the children's daily lives. Lim Han-ci, if one can believe the stories of his neighbors and children, was far more active in the training and control of his family. His treatment of his children is the subject of many of the village anecdotes about his life. Lim Han-ci demanded of his children the same hard work he demanded of himself; he made no allowances for high spirits or play; and he was considered strict in a community where children are punished severely and often cruelly. Lim Chieng-cua admitted that his father had once in a moment of anger beaten him and his older brother with the heavy wooden handle of a hoe, covering them with bruises that stayed for weeks. His father's more formal punishments included taking the misbehaving child down to the river and dunking him several times.

Lim Han-ci's reputation caused as much, if not more, terror to the other village children. An historian who grew up in Peihotien said he often walked half a mile out of his way to get to school without passing a field in which he had seen Lim Han-ci working. The bunds that enclose each small paddy field and keep the water on the growing plants were (and still are) a constant source of dissension between farmers and children. In some places pathways serve as natural bunds, but in others they are painstakingly built up with earth. Being only a foot and a half to two feet wide, they are delicate; a bit broken off an edge might easily begin an erosion that in a night could empty a field of its precious water. Imagine a vast network of bunds and a child in a hurry. Lim Han-ci prided himself on keeping his bunds squarer and freer from weeds than any other farmer in the area, and woe unto the child who trespassed. A child who made use of one of Lim Han-ci's bunds without being caught would nonetheless run from him for weeks afterwards. Laughing at his own youthful terror, Lim Chieng-cua told me he once saw his father cut down a piece of bamboo to repair a fence but was so convinced that he was to be beaten with it that he hid for hours in a deserted field shed.

After hearing these and many more tales of Lim Han-ci's sever-ity and the uncompromising demands he made of his impoverished family, it was difficult for me to understand the genuine affection with which Lim Chieng-cua and the other members of the family spoke of him. Perhaps adulthood brought them a greater understanding of the things he was trying to do for them and to teach them; perhaps too their fear of him was tempered by pity when he received what must have been the greatest blow of his life. At nineteen, Lim Hue-lieng, the eldest and therefore the favored son, revolted against the unyield-ing discipline of his father and left the family home. Lim Han-ci was not a man to be broken by this—even to the day of his death the children who remained behind were afraid to cross him—but he learned to soften his commands and to allow for needs he himself did not feel. As his neighbors say, "Something was missing after that."

When Lim Han-ci was dying, the family took an unusual step for villagers. At that time the countryside had few doctors. To be sure the old man had the best treatment available, his children took him to a hospital in Taipei. "But," Lim Chieng-cua told me, "he found out how much it cost and refused to stay there. We were all so afraid of him that we couldn't do anything other than bring him home again. We had a doctor fetched to Peihotien every day in a cab and each time warned him not to let my father know he came all the way from Taipei in a taxi. We spent a fortune in that last month, but he worked hard for us all his life."

Lim Han-ci's funeral was the biggest ever seen in Peihotien and his daughter-in-law claims it was one of the most expensive in the whole district. The coffin alone cost NT$3,000 and the family spent another NT$1,000 to hire musicians. Taoist priests were summoned to chant both day and night as long as the coffin remained in the house. Nearly two hundred guests sat down to the funeral feast. When I asked Lim Chieng-cua why so much money was spent on these final rites, he answered my question, but obliquely. "Many people correct their old parents when they are still alive, saying 'This is old fashioned,' and 'That is no longer done,' but when their parents die they discover how good the old people were to them and wish they were still alive to advise them. People have to give a big funeral for their parents when they die for the sake of face. If they don't, other people will laugh at them. But really, it is the one time that the children can express the respect they feel for these people who have worked for them all their lives. There is no other way to do so."

Lim Chieng-cua and other members of the family credit their present prosperous and respected position in the community to the work of their father, but most of their neighbors have a different explanation. The villagers have made as much of a legend of Lim Hue-lieng, the eldest son, as they have of his father. In purely financial terms the Lims' present income probably did result from the benefits they received when Lim Hue-lieng's career was at its height. Lim Han-ci was only a farmer, after all, but he was a shrewd farmer and knew how to use the things that his eldest son later placed in his way. In another sense Lim Chieng-cua and his family may be right. Lim Han-ci's good judgement and severe honesty brought respect to himself and to his family. Harsh as his training may have been, he taught his children to aim for and achieve standards higher than their neighbors, to accept their responsibility to the community without becoming involved in its squabbles, and above all else to work hard for what they wanted. It was this training that led Lim Hue-lieng to his success in the world outside Peihotien.

chapter 5

LIM HUE-LIENG: AN ELDEST SON

Lim Hue-lieng entered this world as the first son of his parents and the first grandchild of his grandparents. His birth was thus almost certainly a matter of great joy in the Lim household. His mother's isolation as a daughter-in-law was now at an end: until a woman bears a male child she is only a provisional member of her husband's household, merely a daughter-in-law; with the birth of a son, she becomes the mother of one of its descendants, a position of prestige and respect. The birth of his first son must also have been a moment of significance for Lim Han-ci. A man with a son becomes a link in the long chain of descent. His struggle with the land for enough to eat takes on new meaning: he will one day be the head of a household, the senior representative of the family, no longer an adult child living under the authority of his father. And if the birth of their first male child is a matter of rejoicing for the child's parents, the birth of their first grandchild is even more of an eventful day in the lives of the child's paternal grandparents. The joy of every elderly Chinese is to spend his declining years in the company of his grandchildren, and it is a matter of great pride for a man to know that he has grandsons as well as sons "to see him to the mountains." They are tangible proof that his line of descent will continue, that offerings will always be laid on his ancestral altar, and that the work of his own life will be multiplied in its benefits. More than anything else, they stand as evidence that these people have done their duty to their own parents and grandparents.

We can thus be certain that Lim Hue-lieng was spoiled as a child. All Taiwanese boys are indulged and pampered for their first six or seven years, and first-born sons often enjoy special treatment even longer. Married to the stern, ambitious Lim Han-ci, Hue-lieng's mother probably had neither the time nor the permission to spoil him as much as other mothers might, but grandmothers need ask no permission—even from sons like Lim Han-ci. A man's children belong to his own parents before they belong to him. Parents do not come into full rights over their children until their own parents die. Like every child fortunate enough to be born while his grandparents are still alive, Lim Hue-lieng spent much time in their company. His grandfather probably told him stories, took him to the store for treats, gave him affection openly and without the reservations necessary for maintaining authority; his grandmother protected him from parental discipline, saved food for him from the table, and shared her bed with him. If Lim Han-ci resented this indulgence of his son and thought it unwise, the unfortunate consequences of the situation did not teach him restraint and wisdom with respect to his own grandchildren, whom he spent much of his time spoiling in the last years of his own life.

Like all members of the Lim family, Lim Hue-lieng grew up into a strong, willful personality; he had in greater measure than most the family's fierce temper and their independence. As a child he feared his father's punishment; as a youth, he resented it; as a young man, he looked outside his home and found that there he too could be respected, feared, and obeyed. He and his father were soon in conflict over his outside activities. The more his father attempted to restrain him, the more satisfying Lim Hue-lieng found life outside his family. He became a leader among the young men in Peihotien, and before long was recognized as a leader by the young men of the whole Hotien area. His name was being mentioned by people who had never heard of the village of Peihotien. At the age of nineteen, Lim Hue-lieng left the family home and severed his relations with his father.

To the Westerner accustomed to adolescent revolt and the approval of independence in young men, this may seem like an entirely reasonable and justifiable action. In the social context of Peihotien in the 1930's, it was an act of extreme moral violence. A Chinese son's first duty is to obey, respect, and support his father. Children exist for the sake of their parents. When a Chinese son dies before his father and thus is unable to take care of him in his old age, the father is expected to ritually beat the coffin at the funeral, "to punish the child for being so unfilial as to leave his father alone in his old age." One can imagine what the reaction of a man such as Lim Han-ci must have been to this open and public revolt on the part of his son. His neighbors condemned the boy as unfilial, but for Lim Han-ci this held little solace. It only increased his humiliation. Rather than accepting the exoneration of his neighbors, he recognized his failure for what it was. With his remaining children he struggled, with some success, to soften the harshness of his character.

The very fact that Lim Hue-lieng dared to defy his father and set out on his own is evidence of a confident, stubborn personality. He had no money to buy land and establish himself as a farmer, and what few jobs were available in factories and shops usually went to the relatives of the proprietors. Lim Hue-lieng was able to assert his independence without economic disaster because of the unusual qualities of leadership he possessed and the position he was building for himself in the *lo mua*. The *lo mua* is a purely Chinese institution for which it is difficult to find a Western parallel. I am tempted to call it an organization of gangsters because of its methods, but since many of its goals are to uphold the traditional morals of the society, the parallel is specious. The *lo mua* contribute heavily to the repair of temples and to the expenses of religious festivals. They have been known to severely punish outsiders who, from ignorance or poor judgement, suggest lewd activities to respectable women of their area. They frequently protect the down-trodden for no charge, and just as frequently force their protection on the wealthy at near ruinous prices. A business man on bad terms with the *lo mua* may find his shop robbed weekly while his neighbor who is more careful in his relationships hardly need lock his doors at night.

The details of Lim Hue-lieng's career between the time he left his father's home and his reappearance there in his late twenties are known only by way of gossip and hearsay. Probably no one knows all the steps in his career, but by the time he was twenty-five, he had established his leadership over all the *lo mua* in a large section of the Taipei basin, and his influence was felt in the Taipei market place, reputedly the center of *lo mua* activity. I know that he had been jailed a few times, but was always promptly released; that he had been in hiding several times, whether from the police or from rivals I am not sure; and that by his late twenties he was considered an important man. During this time he was no stranger to Peihotien, but he did not enter his father's house as a son. The villagers followed his escapades avidly, particularly his romantic attachments, since the women in his life were many and most were far from respectable. For the village youths and even their sober parents, he came to be pictured as a kind of Chinese Robin Hood.

In describing Lim Hue-lieng's early career, an eminently respect-able old farmer told me, "Lim Hue-lieng started out as the leader of all the *lo mua* in this village and then of all the other villages around here. He and the other *lo mua* from here used to fight a lot and they were so famous that even now no one dares to do anything to hurt this village. If someone made a comment about somebody's walking too close to one of our girls, they would fight them right away, or if someone said something in public they would set a time and fight with them later. And if they heard a man was coming to our village to visit a prostitute who lived here, they would wait for him on the path and beat him up. They did all of this to protect the good name of the village.

"They were also famous for 'squeezing the oil' from gamblers and made a lot of money protecting the houses and names of wealthy families in Tapu. Those *lo mua* didn't have to use force. If they wanted money, they just asked someone to loan it to them, and the person didn't dare refuse."

Even the peaceful, quiet men of the village who abhor the kind of life Lim Hue-lieng led are willing to admit that there is still an aura around the name of Peihotien that causes thieves to pass it by. Ameri-can friends in the well-policed city of Taipei maintained elaborate systems of locks and watchmen, but were robbed repeatedly. We left expensive cameras, typewriters, and watches scattered about our un-locked rooms and never lost so much as a pencil. The petty *lo mua* activities of today's young men are as disapproved by the older and more stable elements of the population as they were thirty years ago, and perhaps with more reason since there seems to be considerably more fighting and far less activity in support of the community and traditional morality. Peihotien's reputation provides the young men of the village with a high status among their peers, but it also demands that they maintain certain standards. They are less able than other youths to ignore a slight or an insult.

During the prime of his life, Lim Hue-lieng's activities were more open. Because of his position in the *lo mua*, he was able to round up gangs of workers on a moment's notice. It was from this source that he received the majority of his income: as long as a man remained on the job Lim Hue-lieng found for him, a certain percentage of his wages went to Lim Hue-lieng. Since his loyalty to clansmen and friends was strong, Lim Hue-lieng's power had a profound effect on the prosperity of Hotien. Besides finding jobs for fellow villagers, he contributed generously to village festivals and community projects such as road building, and he built the lovely Tu Ti Kung shrine that graces the entrance to Peihotien. Without this patronage, Lim Hue-lieng's reputation in his home village would not have been good. Against him remained the stigma of being an unfilial son. And still unmarried in his father's home remained Lim A-pou, the girl his parents had adopted to be his wife. Lim Han-ci made no attempt to arrange another marriage for the girl, and she was rapidly approaching the age after which it would be difficult for her to make a good match. When Lim Han-ci's wife brought home a small girl and Lim A-pou took responsibility for the child's care, there was no longer any doubt in the village about A-pou's future. She was not to marry out of the family. If Lim Hue-lieng did not marry her, the child was to be the most Lim Han-ci could do to provide his eldest foster daughter with support in her old age.

To make a story suitable for the textbooks of Chinese youths, Lim Hue-lieng at the height of his career should have come on his knees to his father, poured riches into his lap, begged forgiveness, and forever after submitted to his father's will. The Lims are not made that way. Lim Hue-lieng and his father were too much alike, and in all the wrong ways, for them ever to live together in harmony. Hue-lieng continued to bear the public stigma of an unfilial son, but he never really did abandon his father. As his own prosperity increased, so did that of his father's family. He could not submit to his father, but he could and did see to it that his father invested money in the right enterprise at the right time. If the enterprise failed, his father never heard of it. During these years Lim Han-ci did not speak of his eldest son and if they ever met, no one knew of it. No one in Peihotien had any reason to believe it would ever be otherwise until one New Year's Day Lim Hue-lieng walked into his father's home and underwent the simple ceremony required to transform foster siblings into man and wife. Considering his prosperous independence, this step in itself was as exciting to the villagers as would have been the traditional return of erring sons in Confucian tracts on filiality.

Why did Lim Hue-lieng choose this way of publicly reinstating himself in his father's home? The least generous answer might be that at that particular moment he had need of a respectable tie, a semblance of a stable family background, and that his father had set the marriage as a formal act of contrition. Considering the nature of Hue-lieng's power, this seems unlikely. More likely his decision came from a growing maturity that allowed other elements of his personality to take precedence over his glowering independent pride. His respect for the traditional mores of his society had threaded its way through all of his *lo mua* activities, had prompted him to keep Hotien as the base for his life rather than to move into the gayer world of the city, and had maintained his loyalty to relatives and friends. He had rebelled against his father's domination, but in his own way he respected him. His rebellion had not altered his affection for his mother, nor for his younger brother, although the latter out of loyalty to his father was sometimes cold and hostile to Hue-lieng's overtures. And perhaps Lim Hue-lieng felt pity for the desolate future of A-pou if she had no position in the growing family beyond that of unmarried adopted sister.

Unlike the elaborate feasts and festivities that mark the marriage of two unrelated adults, the wedding of foster siblings is a quiet ceremony witnessed only by members of the family and perhaps a few other relatives. In recent years, this form of marriage has almost completely disappeared from Taiwan. Parents find in it many advantages, but the young people themselves loathe it. Nowadays when jobs outside the village give young men more bargaining power with their parents, they refuse to marry their foster sisters. Their objections are primarily to the sexual aspect of the union. In China, as in the West, sexual relations between siblings are forbidden. Sexual intercourse between two people who, though unrelated, have called themselves and behaved as brother and sister all their lives seems "wrong." The social technicality that condones such relations between foster siblings is not sufficient to overcome their revulsion. Since Lim Hue-lieng expected to continue his life in the outside world where "normal" sexual activity was readily available, perhaps the incestuous feelings that make such a marriage unbearable to others did not worry him.

As a point of fact, Lim Hue-lieng's marriage had little effect on his daily life. He did not live in the family home and took no interest in their daily activities. The marriage did, however, add one more chapter in the growing legend of his great personal power. He became the hero of one of the most popular village tales of sexual prowess. It was his boast and the favorite story of his admirers that he spent only two nights in Lim A-pou's bed: on his wedding night he gave her Lim A-bok, and some years later when a typhoon forced him to spend the night in the village, he gave her Masa. The rest of his nights were spent with a series of mistresses of whom even the most salacious village gossips have long since lost track. Finally, when his first-born son was about two years old, Lim Hue-lieng settled down more or less permanently with a village girl, Lim So-lan, the adopted daughter of another Lim family.

Because my assistant came to know Lim So-lan well during our stay in the village, So-lan was willing to tell us quite a bit about her life as Lim Hue-lieng's "second wife": "He only lived with his first wife for a few days just after they were married. After that he never stayed home at night. Before he began to live with me, he had a great many women, but he always left them after a little while because they were just interested in making money and would sleep with other men. When he first came to live with me, I was only seventeen years old. He had just returned from hiding from the police for a few months and had also just broken off with the last woman because she slept with someone else while he was away. His eldest son was about two years old then. He was a good friend of my foster mother, and often joked with her about me, telling her that he wanted to come and live with me. I was working in the river then, gathering rocks, and saw him there every day because he was the head of all of the people doing that kind of work. At that time my family was very poor because my father gambled too much. That year he gave us money to help us through New Year's. My mother was always urging me to marry him. I told her that he was a *lo mua* who had had a lot of girlfriends and would beat me if I did anything he didn't like. I was very afraid of him and ran away every time I saw him. When my mother said that she wanted me to marry him, I cried every night, but my mother knew that he made a lot of money and would help our family, and so finally she asked him to come and live in our house. He lived with our family for five or six years.

"He was very good to our family, and after he came to live with us, my father didn't dare gamble any more. He rented a boat for my father so that he could work ferrying people across the river. The first year he came to live with us, he spent a lot of money helping us because that was the year that my father and my grandfather and my grandmother all died, and he paid for all their funerals. The second year, I had my first child. This was my daughter, Gioq-ki. If it hadn't been for her, I would never have been able to live with him for so long because not long after she was born he began to go out with other women again. I wasn't as afraid of him then and so when I found out he had been with other women I would get mad and fight with him and then he would get really angry and go away. But he always came back, and that was because he wanted to see Gioq-ki. It seems strange that he should love her so much more than his sons [by Lim A-pou], but he did.

"When my younger brother was old enough to earn a living for my family, he moved me into a house in Tapu. He continued to give my family money though until after my brother got married. We lived in Tapu for eight years. During those years, we lived very well because he made a lot of money. He loved to have guests and on special occasions he would buy enough food to open a store. He had so many friends that you didn't know where to begin to count them.

"He could gather up a crew of workers very quickly and he was the head of workers in many different places. He did this kind of work until after the Restoration, and then he went into construction work. He got a lot of jobs moving factories and things like the winery back to where they had been before the war. The Japanese had moved them all up into the hills to save them from the American bombers. He was very much hated by the other people doing this kind of work because he always made the best bids and got the best jobs."

For a man who began with nothing, Lim Hue-lieng had risen far in terms of power and money by his early forties. It was at this time and, ironically, due to the moving of the winery back to Tapu that his career ended. The competition for this job had been more intense than usual, and Lim Hue-lieng's success even more resented. Lim Hue-lieng had probably not been completely fair in his methods because for some reason he agreed to share his profits on the job with some of his competitors. His admirers still prefer to think that this decision was his own, and only another example of his generosity, but this kind of generosity is not characteristic of a man who has risen through the ranks of the *lo mua*. His competitors had more than likely caught him in practices unfair even among the *lo mua*. On the day that he was to divide the money with them, there was a problem. The officials of the winery had to delay their payment. Lim Hue-lieng informed the men of this and they seemed to accept it, even inviting him to a dinner the following evening. Lim Hue-lieng was not paid off the next day either, and when he explained the problem to his "friends," they gave every indication of believing him.

A Taiwanese dinner party is a seemingly informal affair that operates under very formal rules. Even in the village, feasts are rarely simple expressions of hospitality. The guests are poor relatives, wealthy relatives to whom the host is indebted, friends, business associates, and men to whom he owes social or monetary debts. In some families these tend to be quite large affairs with four or five tables of eight men each. There is another kind of dinner party—more common to townsfolk but occasionally given by the wealthier village men— which can only be described as select. These parties are limited to one table of guests and are usually held in a restaurant rather than a home. Each guest is invited for a definite if unspecified purpose: the man who is pressed by his host into the most honored position at the table knows he is being thanked for a favor, or about to be asked for one; the guest who finds himself sitting in an undesirable spot is silently informed that the favor he requested will not be granted; another guest is made to understand that his friendship is valued but should not be pressed by a special request. In Taipei it is common for businessmen to give a feast for their employees during the New Year's season. An employee whose performance has been unsatisfactory will find himself in the honored position: his employer is giving him face before his fellow workers and also making it clear that he should resign the following week.

Be it a select dinner party or a huge village feast, the duty of the host is to urge as much food as possible down his guests and as much wine. Wine drinking at a banquet is the least informal aspect of the whole affair. If he wishes to insult no one (and this may very well not be his wish) each guest must drink a toast to every man at his table at some time during the evening. No guest can refuse to drink the toast without causing serious insult or involving himself in a long explanation. Since drinking in the village only occurs in conjunction with course after course of heavy food, there is little drunkenness, but the goal of the good host is to get most of his guests at least pink-cheeked or his dinner is not a success and his hospitality may be questioned. The businessman or official who has to look in on two or three of these ordeals in an evening learns to shift the favored "drain the glass" toast to a moderate sip. Not to develop this skill invites disaster since it is under these conditions that the major decisions in a man's business life are made.

Considerable planning must have gone into the dinner party for Lim Hue-lieng. He could avoid without offense as many toasts as any man, and he had a reputation for holding his liquor well. Perhaps that evening he was feeling more cautious about giving offense; perhaps, as some villagers believe, his liquor was tampered with; or perhaps he was simply careless. At any rate, he was toasted again and again and proved no match for the concerted efforts of seven men. He was brought home nearly senseless with drink. During the night, some unknown men secretly entered his house and efficiently severed the tendons of his knees, elbows, and fingers. The attack was designed to cripple, not to kill. It was two years before Lim Hue-lieng's wounds healed. When they did, he could neither walk nor clench his fists.

Lim Hue-lieng had loyal followers and friends, but during his long convalescence they necessarily formed new alliances and became involved in other business enterprises. When his injuries healed, it was apparent to everyone that he no longer had the physical strength prerequisite to his former occupations. A man who cannot walk cannot gather up gangs of men quickly, and a man who cannot clench his fists cannot enforce his terms. Lim Hue-lieng sold his house in Tapu and moved himself and his second wife and child back to his father's house in Peihotien.

Lim So-lan told me about those last years with Lim Hue-lieng: "We lived with them for over two years. I had never done much heavy work before, but after we moved there I had to do all kinds of hard work, even in the fields. I cried a lot in my stomach in those days, but I didn't complain. I gritted my teeth and did any kind of work that had to be done, and so his parents liked me, and for awhile we all got along very well. Then my husband decided to adopt A-hua, and that made his first wife angry. She went around telling everybody, 'They can't make any money and yet they go ahead and adopt another child for other people to feed.' She didn't dare say anything about it to him because he wasn't the kind of man who let others tell him what to do, but she said it to all the rest of the family. She hated me because Hue-lieng liked my Gioq-ki and A-hua and didn't pay enough attention to her children. Finally, she caused trouble between Hue-lieng's parents and me. It was because of her that they wouldn't speak to me after he died.

"When Hue-lieng saw that Lim A-pou and I weren't getting along very well, he bought this house I am living in now, and we moved here. This was when he began making wine. He fixed up the house next door and made the wine there. He really was making a lot of money again when the police made him stop."

Lim Hue-lieng's career in wine-making didn't last more than a couple of years. The production of wine was a government monopoly, and his activities were illegal, but he depended upon his former power and the loyalty of his former associates to keep the police looking the other way. Unfortunately, a really successful bootlegger soon comes to a good many people's attention simply by having a product superior to the government's wretched brew. Finally, his friends warned him that investigations were being made by people over whom they had limited influence. He heeded their warnings. Punishment for bootlegging on Taiwan is severe, but Lim Hue-lieng was not even fined. Nonetheless, he was again without an income. He still had many friends who visited him both for pleasure and for advice, and his wits soon turned this into a comfortable living. "After we had to stop making wine," Lim So-lan said, "my husband began inviting his friends here to gamble and that way we were able to earn enough money to live. At that time Gioq-ki had graduated from lower middle school and was studying to be a seamstress, but we didn't have enough money for her to continue studying. Before my husband was making money again with the gambling, a friend found her a job in a newspaper office in Taipei. It was there that she met Chang Jong-kuei. He brought much unhappiness to our family. Her father wanted her to marry a man who would be willing to be our adopted son because we have no sons. Besides that, Chang was a mainlander."

The kind of marriage Lim Hue-lieng planned for his daughter is common enough on Taiwan. The husband comes to live with the wife and her parents and, ideally, becomes more a son to the family than a son-in-law. He inherits whatever property the parents might have given a son and in return supports the parents in their old age as would a son. In some cases the man who makes this kind of marriage even changes his surname to that of his wife. If he doesn't, at least one of his children, usually the first born, bears the wife's surname to provide her family with genealogical descendants who will maintain their graves and carry out ancestral rites.

Lim Hue-lieng had two sons who out of family pride alone would fulfill these duties to him. Lim So-lan, however, had little or no status in his family and without a son-in-law who was obliged to support her, she might very well suffer after his death. And, what was to become of her after her own death if she had no one to provide for her in the other world with offerings from this one? Even if Lim Hue-lieng rejected, as do many young people of the present generation, the literal belief in the life of souls after physical death, he was pained by the incompleteness, the transitoriness, of his second family and wished to provide for it a future, a future which for a Taiwanese exists only in having descendants. His relationship with his sons by Lim A-pou was not close and, at best, formal. That he should wish to give permanence to his second family with whom his emotions and personal loyalties rested is not surprising. Moreover, he was excessively fond of Gioq-ki and he hated the thought of her leaving home.

All of Lim Hue-lieng's objections might have been overcome in one way or another had it not been for the origin of his daughter's suitor, Chang Jong-kuei. Even after fifty years under Japanese colonial administration, the Taiwanese viewed the restoration of their island to the Chinese government as a liberation. Their expectations were not fulfilled. Because of several tragic events followed by innumerable misunderstandings, there exists on Taiwan an attitude of scorn and distrust between the Chinese native to the island and those who came after the establishment of the Communist regime on mainland China. It is not my place here to evaluate either side but simply to point out that Lim Hue-lieng's reaction to having a mainlander as a son-in-law was in no way unusual. When his eldest son heard of the alliance proposed by his half-sister, he was as angry as his father at the shame the girl was bringing to their family. Only the intervention of some wiser friends prevented him from solving the problem in a way that his father might have used at his age, a gathering of *lo mua* friends. A half-brother's anger, however, is of a different sort than a father's. Gioq-ki's father was both angry and hurt. Lim So-lan told me, "Gioq-ki wouldn't pay any attention to her father. He tried everything. When he warned her that she couldn't live at home or at her grandfather's, she answered, 'All right, I won't come back here at all.' She moved to Taipei and lived with Chang. My mother and I cried every day for hours and her father got angrier and angrier. He said he would kill her if he found her. She made his life miserable. He told me once, 'All my life I have been very careful of my family's name and I have scorned other people who did such things as this. Never did I think my own daughter would marry one of them.'

"We hated Chang for tricking our daughter away from us. He knew she was our only daughter and his heart must be very hard that he could steal a family's only child.

"Later my husband's friends told him that he must forget all this and let them get married. We finally had to agree. There was nothing more we could do because Gioq-ki was about to have a child.

"One thing is very strange. My husband threatened to kill Gioq-ki and this man, but after they were married and his grandson was born, he treated them very well. I think he was really fond of them by the time he died."

Not long after the birth of his grandson, Lim Hue-lieng fell ill, evidently from something connected with his injuries. His last illness was long and trying, but it wasn't until his death was imminent that his father had him moved to the family home. A relative of the family told me of those last weeks: "Lim So-lan took care of him all alone while he was ill and during the last stages she was with him day and night. Lim A-pou didn't seem to pay any attention to him at all and acted as though she thought, 'This doesn't concern me.' When Lim Hue-lieng died, So-lan cried for days and days, but his wife, Lim A-pou, didn't grieve at all."

Lim So-lan told me very simply, "The first few months after he died I didn't want to go on living. I spent a lot of time with my mother then. He was very good to my family and even though he was not really my husband, I lived with him for a long time. This year I will have a tablet made and burn incense for him on Ch'ing Ming Chieh."

Very little of my information about Lim Hue-lieng's life came from his younger brother, Lim Chieng-cua. Lim Chieng-cua was quite frank about the various roles the *lo mua* have played in the history of the village and its present affairs. His opinion of them is not always negative, but he always uses the term *lo mua* to refer to a collective group and rarely to a specific person or his contributions. On occasion he pointed out one of our neighbors who had been an active *lo mua* in his youth, or some of the young men who participate with the *lo mua* on an amateur basis; but he never discussed his own family's connection with *lo mua* activities, past or present. At first I accepted this as a device to protect his family, but as the months went by and our staff became more accepted in the gossip sessions of our neighbors, I found that he did not allude to his brother's connections in conversations with others either. I do not believe Lim Chieng-cua is particularly ashamed of his brother's career or that he harbors any deep hatred of him, but rather that as head of the Lim family he intends to maintain for the family the aura of normal respectability his father struggled to create. His brother, even after his career outside the village was ended, never took the responsibility in the family expected of an eldest son. He submitted to a marriage with the girl of his father's choice, but he never really returned to the family. If his career was responsible for the family's sudden rise to prosperity, fate could just as easily have sent some other form of luck. Lim Chieng-cua prefers to have it believed that Lim Hue-lieng was a deviant and not representative of the family established by Lim Han-ci. He wants the Lims of Peihotien to be known not as an obscure family made wealthy overnight by the doubtfully obtained fortune of one of its sons, but rather as an old, well-respected family that came upon better days due to the perseverance of the father.

chapter 6

LIM SO-LAN
A
SECOND
WIFE

About twenty years ago a former villager who still owned a building site in the heart of Peihotien decided that his land should be earning money. On it he built a long brick building that looks very much like a warehouse. He cut four doorways in the front and a smattering of windows and fitted the interior into four separate apartments. Two of the apartments were sold to their present occupants; the other two are leased by families who came to the village within the last ten years. All four families are fragments. They each have an ancestral altar in their guest halls, but two of the altars, though littered with images of gods and ritual paraphernalia, lack ancestral tablets. There are ancestral tablets on the other two altars, but the surnames on them are not the same as that of the family who burns incense before them. The apartments are spacious, in good repair, and in all but one case show evidence of an adequate income. But, the people who live in them are not families in the Taiwanese sense of the word. Their past is not tied to a neat line of descendants; their present is in a house that displays no confidence in the future—wings cannot be added on to an apartment to shelter future generations of married sons and grandsons.

Lim Hue-lieng bought the largest apartment in this row house when he moved his second wife and his daughters out of his father's house. Lim So-lan still lives there with her two daughters, her eldest daughter's husband, and her three grandchildren. She is in her middle forties now and looks her age. She wears the modified Western clothes typical of her generation; once or twice a year she has a permanent wave; she does not wear lipstick or resort to any of the other subterfuges of aging pretty women; she has put on a little weight; she would never be noticed in a crowd. Lim So-lan looks and acts the part of a respectable, middle-aged, village housewife. Even the most malicious gossip in the village can only say of her, "She is a good person. Quiet. Hardworking."

Lim Hue-lieng did not leave his second wife in a very comfortable position. She told me with no bitterness, "We didn't try to save money. We ate very well right up to the day he died." He left her the house, but he also left her with some debts that were either unknown to his father's family or ignored by them. Many women in her position would have refused the bills and sent the creditors to her husband's family, but Lim So-lan chose to settle her own affairs. I heard the following conversation between Lim So-lan's aged mother and a relative from a nearby village.

Relative: "Your So-lan is always busy. She is really a worker."

So-lan's mother: "How can she be anything else? If she didn't work hard, how could she pay off the debts her husband left her? She is always asking people if they need help in the fields. She will do any kind of work."

Relative: "Has she paid that money off yet?"

So-lan's mother: "To the outside people, yes, but she still owes NT$3500 to our family. The thing that really worries her is that daughter of hers, Gioq-ki. Gioq-ki gambles too much and that really makes her mother mad. She usually is the one who has to pay the money that Gioq-ki loses. My So-lan is trying to save some money for herself now. A-hua gives her all the money she makes in the factory, but even though Gioq-ki's children are always begging for pocket money from So-lan, Gioq-ki never gives her any household money. The money the children get for candy is all their grandmother's.

"The only money So-lan owes now is to our family and she doesn't have to pay it back if she doesn't want to. It doesn't matter. She can pay it back if she wants to, but she doesn't have to."

One of Lim So-lan's close friends elaborated on the family's finances: "A-hua gives all of the money she earns in her uncle's factory to So-lan. So-lan works at odd jobs too, and the money they make pays for coal, electricity, soap, and things like that. Gioq-ki's husband pays for the family's food. Gioq-ki owes a lot of money

because of her gambling, so So-lan has had to start a loan society to
pay it off. There are twenty-six members in the group and they each
put in NT$100 so she must owe a lot. [Lim So-lan must have needed
NT$2600 or she would not have organized such a large group.] Gioq-
ki's husband won't give her any money because she gambles so much.
They buy their food on credit at Ng's store and then the husband pays
up the account at the end of each month."

It was only toward the end of our stay in the village that Lim So-
lan decided to take up her husband's last occupation. "After my
husband died," she told us, "his friends told me that I ought to
continue having people in to gamble, but I was too unhappy then to
do it. Besides, without a man in the house this is hard for a woman
to do. Then a couple of months ago Song Sin-bin and his friends asked
if they could play cards here and I let them. When they play mah-
jong, each player gives me a dollar. I make about NT$10 a day. I am
supposed to provide the tiles, but since I don't have any, Song Sin-bin
brings his. I have asked him to sell them to me. I told him I was
embarrassed to take their money when I couldn't even provide the tiles.
He said he paid NT$200 for them, but he would sell them to me for
NT$180, so I think that I will buy them. When they play mah-jong, I
don't make much money, but it isn't much trouble, either. When they
play cards, I make much more money—a pack of cards cost NT$ .50,
but the owner sells them for NT$5, and they can only be used eight
times—but it is a lot more trouble because you have to provide things
to eat, too."

A-hua, So-lan's adopted daughter, is in her late teens now. Her
contribution to the family income is not very large. In fact, the only
way a young girl can make a significant financial contribution is to
become a prostitute, and Lim So-lan's family is not poor enough to
require that kind of sacrifice. A-hua could earn more than she does if
she worked in one of the factories in Tapu or Lungyen, but her
mother will not allow this. "A-hua," she said, "earns NT$15 a day in
Lim Chieng-cua's factory. That isn't too bad. If she went out of the
village to work, she would have to have better clothes and take her
lunch. All considered, she probably wouldn't make too much more.
That is part of the reason I won't let her go outside to work.

"A few days ago when the factory was low on work, she and
some of the others went out and found jobs in Tapu, but I won't let
her take it. Her pay is higher than the other girls who work for Lim

Chieng-cua. If she left him now, he might think I put her up to it. I told her no matter what the difference in pay was, I wouldn't let her go because Lim Chieng-cua is her relative and it would be an embarrassment to work for someone else and not for him. She has worked in the factory for four years now. When she started, she only earned NT$4.50. At first her wages only increased by 40¢ each time, but last year she started to get an increase of NT$2 each time he raised wages. That isn't so bad."

For an adopted daughter A-hua's life, by village standards, is not uncomfortable. Her family is better off than half their neighbors, and her mother is kind. Nonetheless, she is an adopted daughter. Her mother, who grew up as an adopted daughter herself, points out succinctly what this status, or more correctly, lack of status, means: "Gioq-ki is not an adopted daughter so she doesn't have to do much around the house and can refuse to do something she doesn't want to do. A-hua might say no, but I still make her do it. That is the difference."

A-hua's life would be very comfortable indeed if it were not for her elder sister. Gioq-ki is imperious, demanding, and well-versed in the obligations of an adopted daughter. She uses her younger sister as a drudge and as a scapegoat for her own frustrations. Their mother does not often interfere, partly because she is afraid of the temper Gioq-ki inherited from her fierce father, and partly because she accepts her treatment of A-hua as the fate of an adopted daughter. She is far too kind to allow any of the physical cruelties that used to be inflicted on adopted girls, but nothing in her world has ever suggested that adopted daughters can expect much more than this. One day when I was visiting in the large compound of Lim So-lan's mother's family, A-hua came running in, her face streaming with tears, looking for her mother. It was unusual to see A-hua upset—in general, she is a stolid, uncomplaining girl who bears her sister's arrogance patiently.

So-lan had stepped next door for a moment. The other women of the compound tried to calm A-hua as she poured out her troubles. "Gioq-ki told me to give Bun-iek [Gioq-ki's three-year-old son] a bath, but when I got his clothes off he kept saying the water was too hot. Really it wasn't hot, it was already too cool. But he kept insisting and so I said, 'All right then, if you won't take your bath, I'm going to take mine first for a change.' This usually makes him change his mind. Gioq-ki heard this and got mad and started shouting at me to give him his bath first. I went to get some more water to cool off the bath water and I accidently banged the dipper against the tin. It made a loud noise and Gioq-ki began to scream at me. She said I did it because I was angry and I had no right to be angry. She scolded on and on and told me over and over to get out of the house and go live somewhere else. Finally I just said I would come and find mother and if she said it was all right, I would go away."

A-hua's grandmother interrupted her. "You dummy. Gioq-ki is not your mother and yet you talk about leaving because she says to. If your mother said that, it would be different. Gioq-ki isn't your mother."

The other women murmured agreement with the old woman, but A-hua hardly seemed to hear them. "I know why Gioq-ki says these things all the time now. The factory has been closed down for a couple of weeks and so she thinks I am just sitting at home eating her food. Everyday I have to bear her scolding now. When she feels like hitting me or scolding me, she just does it for no reason at all except that she feels like it. She is always saying, 'You are an adopted daugh-ter and I am the real daughter. It is right that I scold and hit you.'"

By this time the room was nearly filled with the various aunts and cousins who lived in the compound, some of whom dismissed the uproar with, "Oh, two sisters always fight." Others, surprised by the unusual break in A-hua's stoicism, tried to console the girl with vari-ous formulas. One of the younger women whispered to me a fact I already knew: even when A-hua puts in a ten-hour day in the factory, Gioq-ki expects her to feed, bathe, and wash clothes for her three children.

When A-hua's mother returned, the girl was still sobbing. One of the women teased, "Oh, here you are, So-lan. Where have you been hiding? You left and let your two daughters quarrel." So-lan had had enough ill temper in her own home and was noticably irritated at finding the confusion in her mother's home. She listened impatiently to A-hua.

So-lan's mother, a wrinkled old lady who hobbles about on tiny bound feet, and who had also been an adopted daughter, intervened. "Isn't it true what she is saying, So-lan? Don't I often see Gioq-ki scolding her and even hitting her without reason? Isn't it time you scolded your Gioq-ki?"

Lim So-lan hates scenes of any kind and her mother's criticism brought tears to her eyes. In attempting to hold back her tears, she answered more sharply than she intended. "You know I have no control over that one. If you can control her, why don't you go scold her yourself."

This made the old woman angry. "You, her own mother, can't control her so you ask me to do it for you!" With that, she scornfully turned her back on the miserable So-lan.

This cast a more serious light on what had started as a squabble between two daughters. The room became much quieter. In a corner A-hua was sobbing to a sympathetic aunt, "She said she was going to hit me, so I just told her to go ahead. She picked up the towel and hit me over and over with it, even in the face."

Lim So-lan's composure failed. "If they keep on fighting like this I am the one that is going to leave and let them fight by themselves. There is no point in my being there. The older one never would listen to me and now the younger one won't listen either. I only have two and all they give me is trouble and fighting. Everyone knows that it is impossible to control Gioq-ki and always has been. I tell A-hua not to make things worse by quarreling with her and her children, but she doesn't listen to me any more. She scolds back at her and reprimands the children in front of her. Even my grandchildren bring me grief. The oldest [a five-year-old boy] scolds me to my face, but I don't dare hit him because his mother wouldn't be happy about that, not a bit! If she gets angry when I, the grandmother, hit the children of course she won't let you touch them. Why can't you just accept this? Just ignore them and listen to me. Oh, that I only have two and one can't be controlled by anyone and has to boss everyone else . . . and now the other one can't let someone scold her. How is there to be an end to the fighting in my house?"

A-hua was too near hysteria to hear what her mother said. In the pause that followed So-lan's lament, A-hua repeated what had almost become a chant, "I know why she does it. It is worse now and I know why. Just because I'm not working now she thinks I am sitting home eating her rice. That is why she does all this to me."

Evidently Lim So-lan had not grasped this aspect of the quarrel. Her despair turned at once to anger. "What is this? What do you say? Is she saying that? No, you are not working now, but it costs her no money. I am the one who pays all the money out in this family, even her bills. How can she say that? When did she say that?"

A-hua was too deep in her misery to comprehend the direction of her mother's burst of anger. She continued to sob, "Oh, if only you had let me take that job last summer. I'll find a job somewhere else. You just tell me how much money you want and I'll send it home every month. I don't want to be at home anymore. It is too much now."

Lim So-lan looked exhausted. She sat down next to her daughter and told her sadly, "All right. If you find a job, I'll let you go. You don't need to send any money. If you want to go, go. I'm going to sell the house and let you two make your own lives. I want no more of this noise and turmoil. I am old now and I want peace."

A-hua was frightened by her mother's weary resignation. She whimpered, "She always says she hated me since I was a child."

Lim So-lan's old mother found she was missing too much with her back to the group. She rejoined them, muttering angrily to her daughter, "That is true, So-lan. Gioq-ki says it to anyone who will listen. She didn't like A-hua from the time she was adopted."

So-lan just nodded without comment. The other women began to drift out; the excitement was over. As I left I heard one of them giving A-hua the age-old consolation: "Never mind. Never mind. In a few years you will be married and won't have to bear her meanness any-more. Just be patient. They will find you a husband soon and then there will be two families, and she won't be able to order you about."

Nothing came of A-hua's outburst. When the factory reopened the following week, she returned to work as an obedient daughter should, and she continued to be servant and scapegoat for her elder sister. I have included the episode here not because it was a turning point in A-hua's life, but because it illustrates how different Lim So-lan's life is from the happy, peaceful existence expected by women with married children and grandchildren. Her husband's anxieties about her future were justified. So-lan's daughters give her little com-fort and her relations with her son-in-law are at best distant. "I never speak to Chang," she said, "partly because I can't speak Mandarin, and partly because I have never forgiven him. He never speaks to me either except to ask me where Gioq-ki is when he can't find her."

Gioq-ki is certainly the cause of most of her mother's unhappi-ness, but life has not fulfilled all the promises it seemed to offer Gioq-ki either. She is, or could be, an attractive woman—tall, graceful, intense. In her mother's face one can still see the gentle prettiness of a former village beauty, but Gioq-ki is of another type. She resembles far more her half-brother A-bok and her uncle Lim Chieng-cua than her short, stocky mother. From her father's family she inherited the unusual long, thin face with its high cheekbones, narrow nose, and firm, somewhat pointed chin. She also inherited, or imbibed, that family's hot temper and fierce character. In Lim Hue-lieng, his brother, and his father, these traits were awesome and even admired; in a Taiwanese female, they are labelled insolence. Gioq-ki is better educated than most village women and though overly proud of her education, she makes no use of it. She is clearly intelligent, but her quick mind only intensifies her restlessness and her dissatisfaction.

It is not difficult to see why Gioq-ki was attracted to the newspaper reporter who grew up on the mainland of China. Chang Jong-kuei is handsome, assured, and sophisticated. His carefully tailored, imported business suits look out of place on village paths, but he shows no signs of self-consciousness. Although the expression on his face suggests affability, his only contact with his village neighbors is at the gambling tables. When Gioq-ki met him, her experience with sophistication was limited to the practiced posing of young village toughs. While bold in a fight and defiant of their enemies, these young men withered at a glance from her father. They speak with confidence and respond quickly to any insult, and yet they are cautious of public opinion in their villages and accept the dictates of local custom. Chang Jong-kuei knows nothing of these restraints. He is an educated mainlander, a city dweller without obligation. Gioq-ki saw him move with ease and assurance through expensive hotels and restaurants in which her father would have looked out of place and slightly uncomfortable. Her father and the *lo mua* feared no one but deferred to the community; Chang Jong-kuei knew no community. The average villager would not trust Chang simply because he is not subject to the usual social pressures, but to Gioq-ki, living in the glow of her father's reputation for independence and power, Chang Jong-kuei's freedom from restraint looked like a personal quality.

At the time Gioq-ki and Chang met, young people in the villages were just beginning to demand the right to choose their own marriage partners. The objections of Gioq-ki's parents to her choice were balanced by her contemporaries' admiration of her boldness. What doubts she herself may have had about marrying a rootless mainlander were cancelled by her fiance's confidence and his dangerously foolish belief in her father's inability to interfere. It is hard to imagine just what sort of future Gioq-ki envisioned for herself, but obviously it has fallen short of her expectations. Like many Taiwanese, Gioq-ki now attributes her misfortunes to fate, *mia*. When one of our assistants announced her intention of marrying a mainland soldier, a marriage of which we thought poorly, though on other grounds, Gioq-ki warned the girl against taking such a step. "You can see from the newspapers that all of the bad things are done by mainland soldiers." When reminded of her own marriage, Gioq-ki answered bitterly, "I was blind and that is why I chose him. My *mia* was like that and so I had nothing to say about it."

The early quarrels between Gioq-ki and her husband arose out of Gioq-ki's insolent refusal to obey anyone, her volatile temper, and her growing habit of spending long hours and not a small amount of money at the gambling tables. Although Gioq-ki was first exposed to gambling during the time her father was running a gambling house, the disease is endemic among certain Taiwanese women. Many of them learn of its hypnotic fascination when they work as wine house girls or prostitutes; others discover it during New Year's festivals when it is almost a standard part of the celebrations. All the women addicted to gambling have a restlessness, a dissatisfaction with their lot, and a pride that has been one way or another trampled on. Once "infected," women ignore their children's needs, use precious food money to buy into a game, and sell anything to continue playing, even their daughters. If their husbands are not also infected, the periodic quarrels between them echo through the village. For a few days after such a quarrel a woman may try to avoid whichever village house has a game in it, but soon she is slipping in the back door with a few dollars clutched in her hand. A gambler in a Taiwanese family can be, and often is, as disastrous as a chronic alcoholic in an American family. Gioq-ki's mother told me, "Gioq-ki often quarrels with me because I tell her not to gamble. She ought to listen to her mother, but she doesn't. Her husband knows she gambles all the time so he doesn't give her money the way he used to. This makes her mad so then she quarrels with him, too. She treats the rest of us badly, but she is a little afraid of her husband. When she quarrels with him it is not as bad as when it is with me."

I stopped by their house one morning and heard a neighbor teasing Gioq-ki about one of these quarrels. Chang Jong-kuei had come home feeling ill, and his wife was in another house in the village gambling. He sent someone to call her home several times, but she delayed. When she finally returned, he slapped her and scolded her roundly. "I tell you not to go out and gamble, but you pay no atten- tion. Here I am sick and there isn't even anyone to hand me a glass of water. I sent someone to call you, but you wouldn't come back. If you ever do that again, I'll beat you to death."

Gioq-ki, of course, answered him word for word, their verbal exchange disintegrated into a physical one, and the listening neighbors were obliged to enter the house and separate them. Chang left and Gioq-ki stood on the doorstep yelling curses after him.

It was the stereotype of a Chinese family quarrel, from the listen- ing neighbors to the wife yelling curses at her husband's departing back. Gioq-ki took her neighbor's teasing calmly enough until the neighbor slyly commented on her swollen eyes and hoarse voice, "Just like someone who has lost her lover."

This made Gioq-ki angry. "I should have such good luck! Don't worry about me! When he went out, I told him to hurry off and get himself killed."

The neighbor offered a bet to one of her companions that if Chang Jong-kuei wasn't back within three days his wife would be in Taipei looking for him. Gioq-ki told her savagely, "Never! Never! I want to see him dead. Why should I go look for him?"

Chang returned, but the quarreling continued. Gioq-ki told me herself of another quarrel, one of which she seemed rather proud although I found nothing in it of credit to her: "Last night when I just had a mouthful of rice yet to eat, A-hua came in with the baby who was crying and crying. I told her to get him out of there so I could finish my last mouthful of rice in peace. She answered me rudely, 'I tried to make him stop crying and he won't. He wants to eat.' Her rudeness made me mad, but I just asked her to speak lower. She shouted again and asked, 'How low do I have to speak?' This really made me mad because at the same time my husband started scolding me, 'You never try to eat a little faster and just sit there and let my child cry and cry.' And then my grandmother came in and had to say something too, 'You are always making her take care of your children so how can you sit and scold her like that?' My mother heard all this so she came in from the kitchen and said, 'It is your own child who is crying, and you don't do anything about it, so how can you go around and scold someone else who is trying to help?' This was just too much. Without even finishing my rice, I grabbed the baby away from A-hua and took him into the bedroom, spanked him, and threw him on the bed. And then I came back and said to all of them, 'You are all just hoping I will leave so I'm going to go away and make you happy. I'm going to go kill myself, and then the nail will be out of your eyes. Then I won't give any of you any more trouble.' I ran out of the house and I heard my grandmother screaming, 'Stop her. Stop her.' My husband came running out after me, but I really ran fast and was all the way down to the big road before he caught me. I was planning to jump in front of a big truck, or if one didn't come by I was going to go on down to the train tracks. I'm just sorry that I didn't think to hit him with my clogs when he caught me."

This was Gioq-ki still uncowed, still the arrogant, undisciplined daughter of Lim Hue-lieng, but the following spring Gioq-ki learned some things about her husband that destroyed her confidence. Most of my information about this came from Gioq-ki's neighbors and in particular from a young woman only a few years younger than Gioq-ki. "Well, she found out that her husband had a girlfriend, and I guess it is my fault she found out, at least about this one. I went to visit a relative who had moved to another town, a girl about my age. When I arrived, who should be leaving but Chang Jong-kuei. I asked the girl how he happened to be there, and she said he was her lover. She showed me all the love letters he had written her and they are *really* love letters! I feel very sorry for this girl. A few years ago she had a mainland boyfriend who offered to take her to be introduced for a job. Instead, he tricked her into going to a hotel. Because of this, she ended up living with him. She wants to be free of him, but he says he will kill her first. So, she has lots of boyfriends instead. She told me that she doesn't like any of them, including Chang Jong-kuei, but she wants the money so she can run away. She didn't know Chang was Gioq-ki's husband. She knows Gioq-ki from school and felt very bad when I told her. She said that Chang told her he wasn't married and had just graduated from college. She said she would never have been his 'friend' if she had known about Gioq-ki."

Gioq-ki's young neighbor was indignant. Extra-marital affairs are not particularly unusual for men with good incomes, but in a marriage classified as a "love match" and arranged by the young people themselves, much more fidelity is expected. Though more sophisticated than most village girls, my informant shares their view —such things don't happen to the daughter of Lim Hue-lieng. Naturally, she came home and reported the whole story to her mother. It was also written in Gioq-ki's "fate" that she sit in the sun under her neighbor's window that afternoon, knitting. Gioq-ki burst into her neighbor's house and demanded the whole story which, though understandably reticent, the girl and her mother were forced to relate. They warned her repeatedly to ignore the affair "because he brings home your income and you should be careful that it keeps coming. Forget about him, but don't throw away his money." Gioq-ki, of course, ignored them and confronted her husband with his philandering the minute he came home.

The village spent half the night listening to their quarrel. The girl next door told me, "My relative really feels bad about all this. She said, 'What is wrong with Gioq-ki? She is a very smart girl. Why did she marry this mainlander? If I were like her, I would leave him immediately.' I think she is right. I would rather not have any husband at all than one like this. She isn't his only girl friend, either. He has lots of women. Someone from the village saw him in a train station with another woman, too. That is why he doesn't bring all of his salary home."

The girl's mother, a retired wine house girl, added: "It is best not to interfere in a quarrel between husband and wife and particularly this one because Gioq-ki is very much in love with her husband —even though she denies it. But she didn't know anything about all these women. She is really very poor, and he never gives her enough money. I know what his job is, and I know he can make at least NT$1800, but he never gives her more than NT$300. Her uncle told her she must go to Taipei on his next pay day and collect his salary before he does. She is going to do this and that will take care of it. No money, no girlfriends."

Chang Jong-kuei didn't return to the village for several days. Gioq-ki followed her relatives' advice and went to collect his pay at the newspaper office. Since Chang often does night work at the newspaper, he has a small sleeping room in the building. Gioq-ki decided to leave the older children in this room so that he would have to return to the village to bring them home. Her plan did not succeed. She met her husband on the street and there was a scene that ended with the crying children being pushed back and forth between them.

Gioq-ki was further humiliated. Chang did not return that night either. I heard a pathetic exchange the next day between Gioq-ki and her favorite aunt.

The aunt: "Don't you worry about whether he comes home or not. You know when he gets paid so you can just go get the money each month."

Gioq-ki: "Yes, I'll go for his money and if he won't give it to me, I'll leave him the children to take care of. I don't care anymore. But I'm sure he will come back tonight because tomorrow is our eldest son's birthday."

The aunt: "Why do you think he will come back for that?"

Gioq-ki: "Well, he was asking me last week before all this started what day it was. . . ."

Chang did not return for his son's birthday. A few days later, I asked another of Gioq-ki's relatives what the latest news was. She told me, "I haven't been out much because I have a cold so I don't know how Gioq-ki is feeling now about these things. Everyone is talking about them, but no one saw the whole thing or knows whether all of these things are true or not.

"When you look at Chang Jong-kuei, he seems like a man with a good enough temper, but when he gets mad he is really enough to scare anyone. Gioq-ki's temper is just as bad. Her nature is just like her father's—no matter what it is, she has to be the head.

"As soon as a man has a family and his wife isn't there, this kind of thing happens. Gioq-ki has only a small family so why doesn't she move to Taipei and live with him there. He works in Taipei and of course he is tired and sometimes doesn't want to come all the way out to the village. If she really believes all the things people here are saying, and I'm not sure I do, she ought to move to Taipei and see if it is really true or not."

When I left the village a few months later, Gioq-ki had not yet followed her relative's advice, but Chang had returned and seemed to be around more often in the evenings. What has happened since, I have no way of knowing.

The reaction of the women in the main Lim family to Gioq-ki's troubles was that of sympathy, which surprised me somewhat, and non-involvement, which I expected. The men, of course, publicly ignored the situation. Even Lim Chieng-cua's wife, notoriously lacking in sympathy for anyone but herself, felt sorry for Gioq-ki. Lim A-pou was no more communicative than usual, but she did make a few terse comments about Chang's origin and what might be expected under the circumstances. The relationship between Lim Hue-lieng's two families is intriguing. None of the women in the main family are what I came to call "wanderers," that is women who of an afternoon turn up in different houses or at the various gathering places in search of conversation and the latest gossip. Lim Chui-ieng has few friends in the village because of her sharp tongue and her snobbishness. Lim A-pou is too busy and as much as possible keeps her daughter-in-law busy, although the latter manages to slip over to the Ong compound more frequently than her mother-in-law realizes. (The Ongs are distantly related to the girl and served as go-between for her marriage.) The Lim family, however, has far too interesting a potential for village gossip to be isolated. There is a steady trickle of women visiting them, watching Lim A-pou in her ceaseless activity, laughing at her daughter-in-law in her ceaseless inefficiency, and smiling at Lim Chui-ieng in her determined attempt to play the great lady. Not once in my long stay did I see Lim So-lan in the house or talking to any of the women from the house. I could not fail to recognize, however, the honest pleasure on her face when she told me that Lim Chieng-cua had begun to drop into her house now that his friends were gathering there to play cards.

Gioq-ki is another matter. She moves freely through the Lim house, even the sleeping rooms, poking into personal belongings, borrowing knitting needles, much as any other daughter of the family. She is equally relaxed with Lim Chieng-cua, her uncle, as she is with her half-brother, Lim A-bok, but what really surprised me is the ease with which she sits down for a visit with Lim A-pou who has more reason to resent her than anyone else in the family. Gioq-ki's naughty children use the house as freely as they do the house in which their grandmother grew up. More than once I have seen Lim A-pou pick up and comfort the older boy after a fall. During several of the long years of childhood, Gioq-ki considered the house of Lim her home—long before she was old enough to understand the delicacy of her relationship. Her personality is such that she could not bear to know that the house of one of the most important families in the village, a family that is closely related to her, is also closed to her. For once she has had the good sense to move cautiously around subjects that are the source of strain within the main family. She has not openly taken sides with either Lim Chieng-cua's part of the family or Lim A-pou's. I could never lead her or her mother into a discussion of the schism in the main family, and in answer to direct questions I received only cluckings of sympathy. In trying to decide where their sympathies might most reasonably rest, I found myself hard put to come up with a feasible hypothesis. Lim Chieng-cua's coolness to his brother and, until recently, complete disregard of his brother's second wife, should disincline them to favor his side, even though he is the head of the household. Lim A-pou's ill treatment of So-lan and the latter's uneasy compunction at having contributed to Lim Hue-lieng's estrangement from his legal family would not particularly make for close ties with that part of the family either, even though there are undeniable blood ties in the second generation. I was left with a frustrating if dignified lack of information which was not the case with any of the other family fragments related to the Lims.

To the casual observer, Lim So-lan's position in the world is quite good. The quarrels between her daughters and between Gioq-ki and her husband probably attract more attention than do other family quarrels because of the strong personalities involved, but not because they are outside the broad range of behavior considered normal in Taiwanese society. Lim So-lan is respected by all who know her as a woman who works hard, pays her debts, and is not inclined to ease her loneliness with malicious gossip. The family income is sufficient for them to eat well and to dress appropriately. They fulfill their social and financial obligations at the weddings and funerals of relatives and give an acceptable number of feasts during the religious festivals. There is nothing indecorous about the fact that So-lan allows gamblers to use her house since they are not professional gamblers and do not bring in outsiders. Her older daughter's difficult personality is accepted with the sigh that covers most idiosyncracies in the village population. Gioq-ki herself has been far too busy with her own problems to meddle in her neighbors' lives.

But in terms of the main tenets of Taiwanese life, Lim So-lan has been tossed into a side pool that must dry up and cease to be. Her marriage (a term which even the most rigid villager would use to describe a liaison that existed for so many years) was irregular in that the children born to her are not descendants of her husband's family. Lim So-lan has no ancestors and her husband's ancestors are the property of the main family. If Lim Hue-lieng and his wife had married Gioq-ki to a young Taiwanese willing to enter their family as an adopted son and descendant, he could have provided the family with a future in the true Taiwanese sense of the word—a chain of descendants continuing for generations after the personalities of the present representatives are forgotten. Even if Gioq-ki and her husband had given one of their sons the Lim surname, obliging him to make offerings to his grandparents' ancestral tablets, there would have been some hope for a future family. Chang Jong-kuei, for reasons known only to him, was unwilling to give even this solace. Although he let his father-in-law believe that the oldest boy bore the Lim surname, he secretly registered him as a Chang.

The marriage of A-hua, So-lan's adopted daughter, is yet to be arranged, and many childless couples have provided their link between past and future through the marriage of an adopted daughter. But times are changing; couples are making their own decisions about marriage partners; young men are now less willing to make the low prestige marriage that cuts them off from their own ancestors and joins them to someone else's. So-lan had little luck with Gioq-ki and it will be difficult to arrange a good match for A-hua. An adopted daughter's inheritance is always questionable when there is a "real" daughter alive. Due to her own ingenuity and the assumed loyalty of her daughters, Lim So-lan need not worry about support for her old age, but she must be satisfied with a pseudo-family that will end with her death. She no longer dreams of a house that can be enlarged to shelter generations of descendants—an apartment in a row house is her present and she has no future. If after her death anyone thinks to make an ancestral tablet for her, it will rest uneasily on an altar dominated by other surnames—a meaningless piece of wood, a link without a chain.

chapter 7

LIM A-POU: A WIFE AND A SISTER

Lim A-pou was born into a family living on the far edge of the Hotien district near the town of Tapu, but only the earliest days of her life were spent in this home. When she was eight or nine months old, the Lim family adopted her to bring her up as a wife for their eldest son. As the Lims were still poor tenant farmers at the time, one of their motives must have been a desire to ensure a wife for their son. They could not be certain that they would be able to afford the bride price if they waited to acquire a wife for him when he reached marriageable age. The marriage of foster siblings has less prestige than that in which an adult bride is brought into the family, but there is some compensation in the knowledge that a girl raised in the family usually makes a more willing daughter-in-law. Even the wealthy who can easily afford the more prestigious marriage sometimes choose to adopt their sons' wives as infants for the sake of future domestic harmony. The introduction of a young woman into a family almost inevitably results in a competitive and often openly hostile relationship between mother-in-law and daughter-in-law; the girl who enters the house as a child is socialized in the ways of the house and bound to her husband's mother by all the ties of parental affection. She is both daughter-in-law and daughter. The adult bride is forever comparing her present life with that in her natal home, but the bride who grows up in her husband's family has no standards for comparison. She accepts her life because she knows no other.

As a girl and as a young woman, Lim A-pou evinced all the behavior hoped for by families who adopt daughters. She accepted reprimands and punishments without becoming sullen, she did not complain, and she worked at whatever job was at hand with a diligence that must have been impressive to satisfy such a hard taskmaster as Lim Han-ci. Several people told me that the old man was particularly fond of his adopted daughter and often said of her, "Where can you find another person who works as hard as A-pou?" His words are as apt today as they were then. She is always busy, and her activities are always productive. Whether in the fields or in the kitchen, her movements are efficient and purposeful. She can easily manage to cook for their family of fourteen, help her bewildered daughter-in-law care for a sick baby, and still have time to rake over a yard of drying rice every hour. The extent to which the family depends upon her was amusingly, if frustratingly, illustrated on one of the rare days she was away. Lim A-ki, her daughter-in-law, proved incapable of both cooking and attending to the needs of her two small children, and the smell of scorching food brought laughing neighbors in to help and to further the confusion. It was truly a memorable occasion in that Lim Chui-ieng was ordered by her husband to assist by washing down the pig pens, a daily task that takes A-pou a half hour and took the appalled Chui-ieng the better part of an afternoon.

I tried many times, without success, to get A-pou to reminisce about her childhood. She was very helpful in providing me with general information about the customs of adoption and the treatment of adopted daughters, but when I attempted to turn the conversation to her own experiences, I never got beyond a proverb. Once I twisted one of her proverbs into a question and asked, "Is it better to be a daughter or an adopted daughter?" It was a foolish question, but she didn't laugh. She just looked away and answered quietly, "I don't know. I have never been a daughter."

A-pou's fate as an adult was to marry her foster brother, Lim Hue-lieng. If she objected, and it must have been obvious that Lim Hue-lieng would be something less than a husband to her, she kept her objections to herself. There was little to be gained by a protest and much to be lost. Her foster father looked upon the marriage as a formal public statement of his eldest son's return to the status of son. A-pou was fond of her foster parents and saddened by the pain Lim Hue-lieng's desertion had caused them. If she refused the marriage, she would not only add to their pain but would also bring to an end the family's obligation to provide for her. To remain in their house under such circumstances would be unthinkable, but for a young woman of A-pou's temperament, the alternatives were too grim to be considered seriously. Where could she go, and how could she support herself and the daughter they had adopted for her—if indeed they allowed her to take the child with her? There were, after all, many advantages to the marriage. The simple ceremony making her a wife as well as a daughter-in-law would greatly improve her status both in the village and in the family itself. And, as the wife of the eldest son, she would have some control over her own future, particularly as the elder generations began to turn over their authority. Lim Hue-lieng's obvious indifference to her might even be an advantage since he would not be likely to remove her from his parents' home and protection. The abhorrence many adopted daughters feel toward coitus with their foster brothers may not have been as pronounced in A-pou's case. Lim Hue-lieng's long absence and the many romantic rumors circulating about his amorous exploits may have given him enough glamour to cloak if not destroy the familiarity that gives rise to feelings of incest. The security of being the eldest daughter-in-law in an increasingly prosperous family could make up for a great deal of what was lacking in the conjugal relationship.

Whether or not Lim A-pou weighed all these advantages and disadvantages, we have no way of knowing. Her decision may have been far simpler. The only respectable thing for a young woman to do in the first quarter of this century was to obey her parents, and A-pou's desire for respectability was, and still is, intense. It is the key to many of her present attitudes and was undoubtedly the motivation for much of her childhood docility. During my first few weeks in the Lim household, there were so many unfamiliar names to be attached to unfamiliar faces that I resorted to descriptive nicknames in conversations with my husband and staff. Lim A-pou was dubbed "the old lady." When I finally sorted out ages and names and relationships, I was amazed to find that she was not quite fifty years old. Unlike every other village woman her age, Lim A-pou wears the old-fashioned Chinese costume and hair style only seen now on Taiwanese women over 70. Around the village she wears dark cotton pants, hemmed to a clumsy level between ankle and knee, and a white Mandarin smock, sleeveless in summer and long-sleeved in winter. For her infrequent trips to Tapu or nearby temples, she wears dark Mandarin-collared dresses cut so loosely and with such decorous side slits that their generic relationship with the fashionable, clinging cheong-sam of Hongkong is questionable. Her hair is parted in the middle and pulled tightly back into a neat knot low on her neck. It is rarely disordered even in the roughest of farm work because (much to the horror of my modern minded interpreter) she keeps a heavy coating of fat on it.

Lim A-pou's extraordinary old-fashionedness, or devotion to tradition, is not limited to her dress. I found her, as do many of her neighbors, an excellent informant on ancient home remedies, rituals for placating household gods and ghosts, techniques for protecting pregnant women, and for purifying rooms following childbirth. Part of her conflict with her late husband's younger brother, Lim Chieng-cua, results from his introduction of more economical practices in the ceremonies honoring the ancestors. Many families on Taiwan now combine the ceremonies celebrating their more distant ancestors' birth and death days, presenting the expensive offerings of meat and fowl to them all on the same day, rather than repeating the expense for each on their specific anniversary. Besides this, Lim Chieng-cua also abolished the bi-monthly offerings to Tu Ti Kung—a less expensive ceremony but one that has not been celebrated in many households for decades. A-pou bitterly resented these omissions and continued to offer an apologetic bit of incense each night and morning to preserve what to her was at least a semblance of propriety. When Lim Chieng-cua installed the new pump in the house without consulting the almanac, A-pou was angry for days. According to the almanac, the Placenta God was resting in that particular room on that particular day. Through Lim Chieng-cua's negligence, the little god was disturbed or injured, and he took his vengeance on A-pou's grandson in the form of a high fever. Before the fever was finally controlled with an injection of penicillin, Lim Chieng-cua and his nephew, the father of the child, had to endure a week of foul humor, both of them alarmed by the illness and neither of them believing in A-pou's theory of causation.

Due to the indiscretion of the only other person who knew of the event, I learned of Lim A-pou's one lapse from rigid respectability.

This lapse undoubtedly colored, if it did not start, the rift between her and her foster brother, Lim Chieng-cua. One evening before the death of either his father or his elder brother, Lim Chieng-cua walked into a thatch tool shelter in one of the family's distant fields and found A-pou and a hired man in compromising circumstances. He soundly thrashed the hired man who has never been seen in the area since, and then administered the same treatment to A-pou. Exercising his usual good judgement, Lim Chieng-cua did not mention the incident to anyone, other than my informant, thereby saving his foster sister's reputation and his father's peace of mind. The effect this strange incident had on whatever relationship had prevailed between Lim Chieng-cua and his foster sister can only be imagined.

A-pou's marriage, if it may be called that, seemed to change her very little. She chose to ignore her rival. When I asked one of her neighbors how it was that she allowed her husband to bring his second wife into the Lim family home, I was answered with laughter. "He was a *lo mua*. How could she dare to say anything about what he did? You have heard about his temper. When he stamped his foot the noise was like thunder. She wouldn't dare say anything to him."

It has been said that A-pou didn't make life easy for Lim So-lan when she lived in the house but I doubt that her displeasure was ever voiced. However, after the death of her husband and then of her father, people began to notice a change in A-pou, particularly people in the family. Chui-ieng, her sister-in-law, told me bluntly, "Before they died she was quiet, minded her own business, and didn't say anything. Now she is exactly the opposite." Obviously, this is an overstatement, but it comes closer to the Lim A-pou I knew than to the one described to me. She is still quiet and she still minds her own business, but her opinion as to what is her business seems to have broadened. To mind it requires that she speak up, if not herself, at least through her son. As long as her foster father was alive, she was confident that she and her sons would share the family's fortune, good or bad, in the same way as other family members, but many things changed with the death of this strong-willed man. As the eldest adult male, Lim Chieng-cua is the head of the family now, but his foster sister is the widow of the man who would have occupied this status had he lived. When Lim Chieng-cua makes a decision affecting the welfare of the family, he is obliged to consult her. Aside from the personal animosity between them, they speak across a barrier of mis-

understandings. She is an uneducated woman who rarely ventures beyond the village world of her childhood; he is a sophisticated man
who must compete in a business world that is becoming less and less
tolerant of small family enterprises.

Before her foster father's death, A-pou accepted the division of
labor in the family without questioning its fairness. Now she does not.
One day while I helped her prepare some radishes for market, she
talked to me with unusual bitterness: "The money in our family is all
handled by Lim Chieng-cua and his wife. We work ourselves to death,
and they take the profits. Except for the money we make by selling a
jin of this or that to a neighbor, we give them every cent of the money.
If Lim Chieng-cua doesn't see us take out the scales to sell something,
his wife does and tells him about it. Last night Chui-ieng saw me
selling fifty *jin* of radishes and right away she went into the house and
told her husband who came out to see what I was doing. I knew he
came out to see what I was going to get and so even though I had
intended to give him the money, I purposely did not give it to him.

"When A-bok and I used to take vegetables to Lungyen to sell,
we gave all of the money to Lim Chieng-cua except for our train fare
and a few dollars we spent to buy bean curd for our lunch. Chui-ieng
hires someone to wash her children's clothes. We work hard so that
she can take it easy.

"When my father was alive, it wasn't like this. We had fish and
meat on the table every day, and we even had to tell him not to buy so
much food. We bought all of our vegetables. Now we have to eat what
we raise. We used to have three people working for us in the fields,
now we have none. At that time our family could save a little money
each year, but now Lim Chieng-cua always says we haven't enough
money to live on and even has to borrow money. My father gave me
NT$200 every time we sold pigs because I was the one who raised the
pigs. Since my father died, we have sold pigs seven or eight times,
earning NT$17,000 to NT$18,000, and Lim Chieng-cua has not
given me even one dollar. Last time we sold pigs, I told him I wasn't
going to raise them anymore. So I want to see where he will get this
much money now. This year we will make about NT$10,000 on the
peanuts, but it will all go to Lim Chieng-cua. When my father was
alive, he gave me a little money each time we made a sale, saying,
'You have worked very hard so take this money and spend it on
yourself.' Now I can't plan on getting even a dollar for my own use.

When I have to buy something, I have to go and ask Lim Chieng-cua for it."

Lim A-pou is not one of the village "wanderers," but she is less constrained now about airing her grievances to one or two sympathetic neighbors than she once was. She is always careful as to what she says, touching only on disparities that are apparent to all. The extent to which she exploits the villagers' general lack of sympathy with Lim Chieng-cua's wife is adroit. One of my favorite "wanderers," always eager to tell me about Lim family affairs, reflects the none too subtle influence of A-pou in her views: "In the Lim family, the work is divided between two brothers, but now that one brother is dead, that half of the family has it very hard. They take care of the fields but have to give all of the money they earn to Lim Chieng-cua. There is a lot of bad feeling between the two wives, Chui-ieng and A-pou. Chui-ieng always wants to manage everything. When Lim So-lan lived in the house she often suffered from that woman. Sometimes when So-lan was cooking, Chui-ieng would purposely drop sweepings into the food so that the old man would scold poor So-lan. Even A-pou felt sorry for So-lan. Chui-ieng never talks to A-pou if she can help it, and she never faces her fully when she does have to tell her something.

"They ought to divide the family and I don't see why they don't. Maybe there aren't any relatives who can do it for them [i.e., act as arbiters on the division of the property]. Lim A-pou's people work very hard in the fields and give all the money to the family. Lim Chieng-cua manages the cement bag factory. Who knows whether or not he gives the money the factory earns to the family? He had to borrow a lot of money and now the family is deeply in debt. He ought to let A-pou manage the family money and see if she can't do better."

The debts to which this woman refers illustrate Lim A-pou's misunderstanding of the management of the family factory. When Lim Chieng-cua is so fortunate as to receive a large order from one of his contracting companies, he is not paid until the order is filled. Since this might mean two or three months work and his factory workers cannot go unpaid longer than a week without suffering real hardships, he uses both factory accounts and family accounts to pay wages. On occasion he is forced to borrow from relatives to meet any large expenses that might arise in his own family. All too frequently the gossips note the borrowing but not the repaying.

According to their relatives and neighbors, the Lim family could solve all their troubles by simply dividing their property and becoming separate independent family units. The large, extended family living together under one roof and contributing their incomes to a common purse is accepted by all Taiwanese as an ideal toward which every family should strive, but few have been able to maintain this form of family for any period of time. The fact that the Lims have done so makes them uneasy and watchful. Lim A-pou, with her devotion to the old traditions, has until recently been quite proud of this further accomplishment of her family, but as my stay in the village lengthened, it was obvious that she now wished a division of the family, no matter what it cost her principles and pride. Her growing dissatisfaction with Lim Chieng-cua's management of the family is not entirely emotional. She remembers poverty more vividly than the younger members of the family and in her mind it is intimately connected with tenant farming. Land, for her, is the only stable unit in an economy that changes as often and as disastrously as Taiwan's. When she sees income from the land going to pay factory workers, she imagines a day when pieces of land may be sold to enlarge the factory or pay its debts. Recent years seem less prosperous than past years. Better that the property be divided now, while it is still in the form of land, than later, when it may be an intangible piece of the factory. Lim A-pou does not understand nor trust the world in which her foster brother operates.

In her quiet campaign for division A-pou first made sure that she had the sympathy of her neighbors, for the opinions of neighbors have no small influence on arbiters in the settlement of family differences. Then, she began to urge her eldest son to be less compliant in his dealings with his uncle.

How successful she is in exacerbating the tensions already existing between uncle and nephew can be seen in a quarrel I had no choice but to witness. Lim A-bok walked into the dining room, grumbling to himself as he read a letter. "This man! He should be embarrassed to write a letter begging me for cucumbers. If he scorns people so much, why should I pay any attention to him."

Lim Chieng-cua looked up and asked, "What letter is that? Who is it from?" A-bok handed him the letter which he quickly read. "What's wrong with this? What's the matter?"

Lim A-pou came in carrying some buckets and said, "We never let him feed us three meals. How can he do this?"

Lim Chieng-cua, looking confused and a little irritated since the letter was from one of his business associates, demanded, "What do you mean you never let him feed you three meals? Why do you say that? What's the trouble?"

Lim A-pou shrugged and said, "I don't know anything about it. Ask my son."

Lim Chieng-cua gave his nephew a questioning look. A-bok answered it unwillingly. "The last time I went to Lungyen to a festival [to represent the family] I missed the last bus. Even though I was in his house, he didn't say a word, so I had to walk all of the way home [a distance of several miles]."

Lim Chieng-cua, impatient and rather disgusted, answered, "Is that all? Did it ever occur to you how he felt at that time? His house was full of guests and his mind full of obligations. Why didn't you just explain the problem to him? I'm sure he would have asked you to spend the night."

A-bok snorted, "Huh! Explain! He is so suspicious of people that he thought I'd steal all his possessions if I stayed there one night. Have I ever neglected to treat him well when he comes here? This kind of person we can ignore."

Lim Chieng-cua, clearly trying to be patient, explained, "Now how can you ignore him? It is in these little things that you make errors. I am the one that has to be in contact with him all the time and do business with him. You have to think of my relations, too. I am the one that bears our family's responsibility to him. The cucumbers are unimportant things. Obviously, he has the money to buy them any-where. The letter is just a joke and a way of complimenting us on the quality of our cucumbers. He is not so poor that he has to write a letter begging cucumbers from us."

A-bok said nothing more, but as he followed his mother out of the room, his face was sullen and unconvinced.

That evening when we were sitting in the kitchen, the subject of the letter came up again. Lim Chieng-cua said, "Look at it this way. You have given people presents and people sometimes give you presents, too."

Lim A-pou, immediately on the defensive, interrupted him. "We only gave Ong A-giok cucumbers because she often helps us in the fields. We never give them to anyone else.

Lim Chieng-cua answered patiently, "I'm not suggesting that you shouldn't give things to people. You can give things to your friends, and I can give things to mine. Didn't this man ever give things to us? He nearly always brings us a big bag of taste powder when he comes. I didn't ever hear him say it was only for me, did you? A person who wants to run a business outside can't be like this.

"Think about it this way for a minute. Suppose this person really had been very bad to you. And now here he is asking you for something, not you asking him. It is he who would be bringing shame on himself by asking, not on you. You can bring shame on yourself only by not giving it to him.

"You say he would not invite you to stay in his house for one night, but did you explain to him what the situation amounted to? No, you just said you had missed your bus. How was he to know it was the last bus or that there was no late train? He is my friend. If your friend came and asked for something and I wouldn't let you give it to him, how would you feel?"

A-bok had had all the lecturing on proper behavior that he could take for one evening, and he said rather loudly, "All right. All right. Don't just stand there and oppress me about it all night."

This bit of disrespect caused Lim Chieng-cua to drop the tight rein he had been holding on his infamous temper. He yelled at A-bok, "You accuse me of oppressing you! You are the one who is doing the oppressing. Haven't I explained anything to you?"

Evidently the expression on A-bok's face (which I couldn't see) angered Lim Chieng-cua even more, and he moved as if to strike him. A-bok jumped up and ran out of the room. A good friend of the family who had been sitting with us immediately pulled on Lim Chieng-cua's arm and began talking to him in a soothing manner. "All right. All right. This is just a little thing. There is no good in it for anyone in quarreling over it."

Lim Chieng-cua calmed down a little and the friend continued to talk to him softly and unemotionally—a trick this man has that makes him much called upon in the village to settle family disputes. "Don't argue with the boy anymore. He is young yet and still doesn't understand the 'affairs of the world.' You are of an older generation and must not lose dignity by arguing with him. If he cannot understand, just forget it for now."

After a bit, the friend in his role as peace-maker went in to talk to Lim A-bok and his mother. A-pou was scolding her son. "If he wants to hit you, just let him hit you. Why do you run? Let the others see how he treats us."

The friend cut her off and began to speak to A-bok as if his mother were not in the room. "Oh, cucumbers. Cucumbers are nothing special. You grow them yourself. It won't cost you any money. Just give them to him. Why argue over these unimportant matters?"

Lim A-pou muttered angrily, "My son is afraid of Chieng-cua just like a shrimp. Even if he doesn't want to give them away, he will have to."

I asked Lim A-pou later if she thought Lim Chieng-cua would really have struck her son. She scowled and said, "Why not? Last August he hit him." When I probed for more details, she said, "Huh! That wife's slave!" and ended the conversation with her usual response of "I don't know anything about it."

A relative of the family did know something about it and was happy to discuss a topic of seemingly endless village interest. Lim Chieng-cua bought a fancy radio for the family. A-bok came in one afternoon to find it blaring loudly for the pleasure of Le-cu, Lim Chieng-cua's twelve-year-old daughter. Besides telling her it was far too loud, A-bok also pointed out that the broadcast was in Mandarin, a language with which none of them are too familiar, and that she should not listen to Mandarin broadcasts for fear that she pick up something from a mainland station and get them in serious political trouble. Le-cu felt saucy and told him it was none of his business because her father had bought the radio. This made A-bok angry and he said some things about Le-cu's mother and maternal ancestors (i.e., cursed in the familiar fashion). Lim Chui-ieng overheard this, as she does nearly everything, and reported it to her husband. Lim Chieng-cua did not bring the matter up with his nephew until the family confidante and arbiter was present. He explained the exchange to him, in A-bok's presence, asking for a statement as to whose behavior had been remiss. One thing led to another, and A-bok got a sharp clip on the head. The friend told me sadly, "From the time he was a child, Lim Chieng-cua has been very fond of A-bok. The only reason they don't get along anymore is the women between them. A woman's heart is always narrower."

Although the quarrel over the cucumbers seems ridiculous and seemed to flare with little provocation, when viewed in a fuller context, it shows some of the finer qualities of both men. Lim Chieng-cua, though he might have suffered from A-pou's ill humor, would have been well within his rights as head of the family to simply order the cucumbers sent to his friend and business associate. Instead, he chose

to reason with his nephew about the situation and to educate him in
some of the subtle details of social relations, a subject the Chinese
classify with their other art forms. He failed because of his own
temper and because he was not aware of the real reason for A-bok's
anger with the man. A-bok's younger brother, Masa, who is frantic to
get out of the village and into a white-collar job, was sent to work in
this man's pharmacy, a business concern in which the Lim family has
invested a small amount of money. Masa often slept in the shop and
one night, after obtaining the permission of the owner, three of his
friends spent the night there with him. Sometime during that twenty-
four hour period, a small sum of money was stolen from the shop.
None of the boys were out of Masa's sight during their stay, and he
knew them well enough to vouch for their complete honesty. The
owner accepted his statement, but commented tactlessly, "When no
one is here to guard, I don't lose money, but when I have four guards,
the money disappears." This made Masa furious. He went out, borrowed the small sum that was missing, and presented it to the man
who was graceless enough to accept it, still however agreeing to
Masa's innocence in the matter. A-bok has never forgiven the man for
this insult, but he cannot explain his anger to his uncle because relations between Lim Chieng-cua and his youngest nephew, Masa, are
good only when they are out of each other's sight.

As the senior male in his branch of the family, it is from A-bok
that the formal request for a division of the joint family must come.
Lim A-pou, whatever her other faults, is not the kind of woman who
nags. She has nonetheless made it quite clear to her son that she
would be happy to see them set up as an independent unit. A-bok's
reluctance to take this step shows the good sense for which his uncle
gives him too little credit. It also is an example of the pride that even
his mother must admit does justice to his father and his grandfather.
In his youth, A-bok showed some signs of following his father's way
of life. He spent every evening with the local youths and, according to
some, was involved in a certain amount of *lo mua* activity. Because of
his father's career, A-bok's inclinations were taken more seriously
than those of his peers, causing distress to his mother and whispers in
the village. Lim Han-ci, however, turned out to be a much stronger
force in A-bok's life than his father. Lim Han-ci was still a hard
taskmaster in A-bok's adolescence, but his harshness had mellowed—
not yet to the extent of spoiling his grandson as his own father had

done to Lim Hue-lieng or he himself would be guilty of with later grandchildren, but enough to soften his commands and make allow-ances for A-bok's occasional lapses. A-bok learned everything his grandfather knew about farming and was encouraged by him to de-velop that talent for innovation which has played such a major role in the family's history. As Lim Han-ci had been among the first farmers to switch to wet rice farming when the irrigation system was built by the Japanese, so A-bok was among the first to devote large tracts of land to the now profitable truck farming.

According to the village gossips, A-bok was not devoted to a life of hard work until after his marriage, but since this notion is tradi-tional, particularly among females with unmarried near-adult sons, I take it lightly. The fact that he submitted to an arranged marriage without even meeting the girl who was to be his bride was taken by many villagers as evidence that he lacked the spirit and independence of his father and grandfather. Indeed, if he had insisted on choosing his own wife, he would probably have been allowed to. But even today in Taiwan, opportunities for young people to meet and become acquainted are few, particularly if they are not employed outside their homes. The kind of young women that Lim A-bok met through his *lo mua* recrea-tions were not women he would wish to raise his children or care for his mother in her old age. His notoriously independent father had compromised also, and when he made a second choice of his own, it was not from amongst the accomplished women he knew in the out-side world but a quiet village girl. A-bok married the girl selected by his mother and the go-between, and with the birth of his first child, a boy, he settled easily into the pattern of his grandfather's life and gave up the pleasures of his father's.

All of the farmers in Peihotien put in long, hard hours and hire help only when essential. Lim A-bok works harder than any and hires help less often than most. Some say that he wouldn't have to work so hard if he took a few short cuts, but A-bok wants his fields to stand out from the others by being freer from weeds and with neater wind-breaks. In general, he succeeds, but certainly at great cost to himself. I have often seen him nodding over his evening meal, but if it is still light after dinner he goes back to the fields. When the hours of day-light are fewer, he spends his evenings repairing equipment and mak-ing rope. Because of his industry and his reluctance to discuss the family's affairs, he is a difficult person to interview. His mother is willing to discuss certain topics with nearly anyone, but A-bok is even more cautious. There are a few long-standing trusted friends of the Lim family who serve formally and informally as peacemakers and as witnesses. As head of the family, Lim Chieng-cua often waits for their visits to air any grievances. This makes A-bok think of the friends as his uncle's rather than the family's and he hesitates to confide even in them. His mother seems to be the only person with whom he speaks frankly.

I hinted and probed for months before I got so much as an admission from him that there were problems within the family. Finally, my assistant and I came across him in a peanut field glutted with weeds. He was weeding frantically and clearly feeling very low. We spent the afternoon pulling weeds which came out somewhat easier than this interview:

"You have been living in our house for a long time now. I am sure you can see that our family is very complicated. I don't much like to talk about family business. If I told people outside the family, they would laugh and say, 'Oh, so the Lim family has *that* much trouble getting along with each other.'

"Look at this field! I have so many different things to do that I can't finish one before I have to jump to the other one. Since I planted this field, it has only been weeded once, and that's when I hired Ong A-giok to weed it. If grandfather were alive, the field wouldn't look like this. There wouldn't be a single weed and those ragged wind breaks would all be trimmed. It just couldn't be like it is now! It shames me."

We worked in silence for ten minutes or so and then A-bok continued, "If you compare the amount of work done by my family and by my uncle's family, who does the most? You just look around you. Even when my uncle sees that I am so busy he won't tell his children to do some easy job like taking the buffalo out to graze when they come home from school. This is work that farmer's children should do, but my uncle never urges his eldest son to do it. I have this many things to do all by myself, and then I have to do children's work too. What is going to keep the fields from growing to weeds? There isn't anyone who doesn't know how to just sit and receive. If he wants the fields full of weeds, I can do that too.

"The generations before me kept this land always planted and always in good order. How can I let them run down and lie fallow?

People would laugh at me. They would say, 'Huh! Look at the Lims now. In former generations they were so good and now they are just the same as us!' When my father and grandfather were alive, nobody dared to say anything more on a subject after they had spoken. Even older generations came to them for advice. It is because of this kind of a past that I don't like to talk about the family's problems with other people and let them laugh at us."

A-bok's comments were interrupted a good many times as the result of our vastly different weeding speeds. In substance he said: "You saw the quarrel I had with my uncle the other day [about the cucumbers], and you know all about it. I am too easy going. I let people look down on me. I don't know how long my life will be, but even if I don't see it, my children or my grandchildren will see if he [his uncle] treats his own children as 'well' as he has treated me. I just keep my head bowed and go on working. When he scolds me, I don't say anything back if I can help it. Whose temper is worst? My grandfather's was the very worst, but he didn't beat me. My own grandfather didn't find reasons to beat me, but now the younger brother is beating the older brother's children. [To a Chinese this is something like saying the world is turned upside down.] I don't think my uncle's children will just stand there and let him beat them when they grow up. His eldest son has a bad temper, and even worse, he holds a grudge over the tiniest things. Le-cu [Lim Chieng-cua's eldest daughter] will fight with you but then she forgives and forgets. I know what people are saying about me in the village. Some of them think I am right, and some of them think my uncle is right. Like Ong Liong-hong [a family confidante who runs a small general store on the outskirts of Taipei]. He thinks my uncle is right.

"My mother gets more and more angry because my uncle's children have several new sweaters and ours are full of holes. My wife keeps begging me to let her buy a pair of white shoes. I told her she couldn't because I didn't want anyone [i.e., Lim Chui-ieng] to talk about us. So what happens? Everytime my aunt walks out of the door, she has a different pair of shoes on. Yet everyday I hear her complain to you that it is harder for her to get money than for a beggar. So where does this money for shoes come from then? When it isn't her turn to cook, she is always off visiting this one and that one. You can't tell me that you can go visit people in other towns without spending money. Where does this money come from? Does it fall out of the sky?

"When it is my aunt's turn to cook, my mother is always around and she helps her with this and that. When it is my wife's turn to cook, my aunt runs far away and she never helps. She lets her children sit and cry rather than get caught near the work. My wife is slower than the others. Shouldn't Lim Chui-ieng be there to help her a little? Feeding the pigs is a good example. My aunt has never once chopped up the sweet potato leaves for pig food. We don't have many pigs to feed now, but we used to have over thirty. They ate a cartload of sweet potato leaves every day. My mother was so busy chopping that food up and cooking it that she didn't have time to turn around. My aunt never once helped her. Mother isn't as healthy as she used to be. How can she stand to go on working so hard all day long. Yet my uncle says the reason she won't raise pigs anymore is because she doesn't want to bother feeding them. The real reason she wants to quit is this. The last time we sold pigs they should have brought in about NT$8,000, but instead we got only NT$5,000 because we owed the butcher NT$3,000. My uncle was buying pork from him every day. If he bought it for everyone, we wouldn't have anything to say about it, but he doesn't. He buys only the leanest pieces and then they cook it with medicine and he and his family eat the whole lot of it. When he comes back from market, his wife takes the meat and hides it under that new bucket in the washroom. My younger brother has seen them do this too. One day just for fun I yelled to Masa, 'Hurry up and get the new bucket and wash it so we can mix insecticide in it.' My aunt took off at a run to get that meat moved. I didn't really want the bucket, I just wanted to see what she'd do. Masa laughed so hard he had to lie down on the ground."

I asked him if it weren't true that Lim Chui-ieng was not very healthy. She often takes medicines of various kinds. He didn't think so. "Huh! She is just pretending to be sick. Who doesn't know how to do that. If she is not healthy, then no one is healthy. If you have the money, who wouldn't eat tonic [a term for describing meat cooked in wine and rich herbs believed to generally strengthen the body]."

Growing somewhat bolder, I asked A-bok if he found it difficult to get money from his uncle for his personal needs. He answered bluntly, "We don't need to discuss that." After a few minutes, however, he did. "It is this way. When you give him money he is all smiles, and when you ask for money his mouth is very stern. I gave Ong A·giok her wages for weeding the cucumbers only two days ago. She did the work many weeks ago. I told my uncle that we owed her money, but he hadn't done anything about it. I thought he had paid her long ago, and I was very embarrassed. Whenever money has to be given out, it is always like this. Even if I don't ask for any money for three months, he will never say, 'Well, you must need money. Here is some so you will have it when you need to buy something.' "

I asked if his uncle might not think he kept money out for his own use when he sold vegetables. "You can't sell vegetables every day," he said, "and besides he knows enough to guess how much we can get for the vegetables we sell.

" 'Even a shrewd man of great ability cannot get past a pretty girl guarding a gate' [a common proverb]. You can't blame him for all these problems. You have seen how that woman [Lim Chui·ieng] can nag. If she is eating and he comes in from the factory, she puts down her bowl immediately and follows him into the bedroom to talk. If she finds him sitting alone, she will hurry over to ask him about this and that and the long and the short."

By my own observation I knew this to be the case, but it did not fit in very well with some gossip I had been hearing in the village. Hoping A·bok's talkative mood would last, I asked him, "If she treats him so well, why did he go out to find a mistress that time?"

"It was her own fault," he answered. "I really wish they would fight again like they used to." A·bok grinned naughtily. "If it hadn't been for my mother and I, Lim Chui·ieng would have been beaten to death a long time ago. One time in particular it was really bad. Lau Kim·chiok was living in that house where her mother lives now. One night Lim Chui·ieng went over and looked in the window and saw my uncle's shoes in there. She was afraid to do anything by herself, so she got one of our friends to go with her—he was living in our house just then. He went with her, but she didn't tell him where they were going, and when they got there she broke the window. My uncle came out and chased her back to our house, trying to hit her. She tried to go into my grandfather's room to hide, but he wouldn't let her and said, 'I'm not going to get involved in this anymore. You solve your own problems.' She had no place to hide so she came into my mother's room. I pulled uncle away and my mother stood between them. Lim Chui·ieng shouldn't have gotten our friend involved because my uncle was going to beat him up, too. Besides that Lau Kim-chiok had a husband then. He wasn't home that night, but my uncle had to hurry and get a man to fix the window before morning or she would have been in trouble. This woman! How can she cause so much trouble and be so jealous. You know Lim Li-kui often used to come to play mah-jong with my uncle's friends and when her daughter [a prostitute] was home, she would come along to watch. Even this made my aunt mad so now Lim Li-kui won't come anymore."

Later in the afternoon, A-bok talked about his younger brother, Masa. "My uncle says Masa is just in the pharmacy to learn. My mother went to ask him for some money, and he told her, 'You know I would send home money if I had it. Uncle gave me enough money to buy a towel, some soap, and a tooth brush. I have no money at all. I was going to come home and ask you for some.' Masa is not a child now. How can you not give him money to spend on himself? If he asks my uncle for money, he gets at most NT$5. What can you do with that? Masa is nearly grown up. You cannot expect him to come and beg for a few pennies every day. I don't blame him for wanting to go outside to work. He hates farm work. Even last year he wanted to go outside to work, and I had to ask his friends to help me talk him into staying in the village. Masa says he gets angry every time he looks at this family. I had to beg him to pity his older brother working all day long like a buffalo in the fields. It is only to help me that he stayed. But later, he had no money to spend so he wouldn't work. I tried to explain to him that things were different now and that it isn't like when grandfather was alive. I was just like Masa at that age. My grandfather always knew what was wrong when I didn't want to work, and he'd give me some money to spend on myself. Young men don't want to work and have no fun. My grandfather knew how to keep me working. But really the times are different too. Now if you want to run a business, it isn't as easy as it was." A-bok was obviously thinking of his uncle's side of the story here and of the fact that his problems are different from the grandfather's problems. "Look how many of the companies that were really big then have just disappeared now. For people like us, it is better to keep the land. It is security.

"But I don't blame Masa for being angry. When he was a school-boy, the work he would have to do was all decided before he even got home from school: where the buffalo had to be taken to graze, what field had to be weeded, and so on. It wasn't like it is now for Kim-hok

[Lim Chieng-cua's eldest son] not having to do anything. If Kim-hok was bringing honor to the family with his studies, I wouldn't complain about it, but he isn't studying at all. He plays all day long. When I was in the fifth and sixth year of school, I already had to work or the older generations would be scolding me. It wasn't long before I knew what I had to do, and I could do it without being told. Don't think I didn't prefer to play! But, they made me work and I was afraid not to. Children are all this way. If you don't force them to work, then they don't."

A-bok even relaxed enough to gossip about something that seemed to amuse him. "You know, Masa took a look in the account books at the pharmacy, and he says that Uncle has already taken out NT$800 worth of medicine, all hormones."

When I asked why, A-bok laughed and said, "Well, they say hormones are even better than *ginseng* for making you younger. [I think he meant to imply that Lim Chieng-cua was trying to achieve a longer and more energetic sex life.] Haven't you seen him taking shots all the time? He also drinks milk everyday, but then who in his family doesn't? If you say anything about it though, they always say it is because one or the other of them is sick. Our family hasn't the good fortune to have such bad health.

"You know that last quarrel I had with Uncle? If it had been Masa, he wouldn't have yielded and would have fought [physically] with him. Masa doesn't care . . . There was another thing that made Masa really mad. My aunt took all her children to Tapu one after-noon and somehow my son got away and followed them. She bought candy for all her own children and just let my son stand and watch them eat. Now you think about that. Was this 'proper behavior' or not? When her second and third sons were small, my mother took care of them most of the time. They even slept with her. So how can she act this way to my son now? Mother helps her all the time, even now, but she not only doesn't feel indebted to my mother, she thinks that she *ought* to help her. She thinks she ought to do this just like a servant. I tell my mother not to help her. My aunt never helps us do anything. She raises all those ducks and chickens and when they get old enough she won't kill them to eat, but saves them for her own family to eat as 'medicine.' You can see that we don't have very many chickens and ducks even for the big feast days." This is a source of great shame to A-bok's mother who is embarrassed that their prosperous family puts on a show little better than the poorest village family on religious feast days. Even our assistants felt that the Lims did not live up to the standards expected of them in this regard. "If my mother hadn't raised some turkeys," he continued, "my wife wouldn't even have been able to have the chicken broth when my daughter was born. [This refers to a strongly held belief that a mother must have chicken and chicken broth at least three times a day in the first few days following childbirth.]

"What does this family look like? Who can see it most clearly? I think my grandfather could see it clearest even then. We should have taken some chicken cooked in wine to my wife's family home when my son was a month old. That is the custom—he was the first born and a male besides. We do this to announce our happiness. Uncle was in charge of the money then, and he didn't say a word about it, so my grandfather took his own money and sent someone to Tapu to buy the things for him. The people from my wife's family sent many things back and my grandfather made a special point of showing these things to Uncle. Uncle didn't pay any attention to this. Evidently that made Grandfather very angry and one of our friends came to visit him and found him like that. He said, 'It isn't as though A-bok doesn't work for our family. How can we treat him like this? No matter how poor this family may have become, we are not so poor that we are going to starve to death. It is only because A-bok's father is dead that he has to depend on us to do these things for him. If his father was alive, you can imagine how finely these things would be done!' I didn't know about this until after the friend came and told me. He said my grandfather talked and talked, and all the time the tears rolled down his face. The friend was very worried about my grandfather. He had never cried in his life.

"It was my grandfather who started the factory, not my uncle. When they couldn't make wine in it anymore, it just sat there empty and someone came and asked Grandfather if they could rent it to make paper bags. Grandfather said they could rent it if they would take him in as a partner. This is the way it got started. It wasn't my uncle's doing. My uncle should be teaching the younger generation how to run the factory, but he won't. I think he is afraid to let me or Masa know what goes on there. He thinks that if he doesn't let me know anything about how to run the business, he can take it later without any worries." This was the first time A-bok admitted in my presence to any thought that the family might eventually be divided. "But I don't think that will work. He doesn't say anything, so I don't say anything. But if he ever tries to take it by force, I will say plenty. This is left from my grandfather's estate—it is not something my uncle made."

A-bok is deeply in conflict about the future of the family and the decision his mother is urging him to make. From what I know of the family properties and economy, A-bok would certainly not suffer as master of his own half of the estate, and he might be better off. He is not only an industrious farmer, he is also a modern farmer. He is one of the few men in the village who reads the farm bulletins and tries new methods. He speaks with pride of older generations coming to ask his father's and grandfather's advice, but he fails to mention that older farmers now come to him for information on marketing or the new insecticides. In these areas of life he is confident. But, his uncle has always managed the paper work, the taxes, the officials, without bothering to explain his actions to A-bok. A-bok's inexperience makes him uncertain, and his uncle's impatience prevents him from asking for the information that would make the paper work seem less mysterious. He is afraid of his uncle—as are most people. A-bok grew up under an older generation of strong, dominating person-alities—his grandfather, his father, and finally his uncle. He has learned what none of these men have had to learn: to bow his head and go on working. But for A-bok the strongest deterrent from mak-ing the decision to divide the family is contained in the above inter-view when he explained why he could not allow the land to go un-weeded. "They would say, 'Huh! Look at the Lims now. In former generations they were so good and now they are just the same as us.'" Personal pride weighs very little, but family pride is the burden of generation after generation.

In this family of strong-willed, hot-tempered personalities, A-bok's wife, A-ki, provides the comic relief. She stumbles through the midst of family quarrels, oblivious and humming. If she feels the tension around her, she reacts to it by dropping a bowl on her foot or mistaking sugar for salt. Nothing in her mother-in-law's dark looks seems to be able to silence her aimless chattering. After the explosive quarrel over the cucumbers, she didn't wait an hour before asking her husband to buy her some useless item of clothing. Undaunted by his silence, she prattled on, and when he finally vented his anger by throwing a rice bowl at her, her response was, "Now Mother [i.e., mother-in-law] will think I broke another one." She sings at her work and stops working whenever her mother-in-law goes out the door. She has learned, no doubt painfully, to be cautious in what she says to "outsiders," and her loyalty to the family into which she has married is strong and sincere. She nonetheless joins in with great glee when her mother-in-law stages a carefully timed description of the discrepancies which exist between the two halves of the family.

I can't help but wonder how grim old Lim Han-ci would have reacted to the small terror that is A-bok's son. Although only three years old, he picks fights (and often wins them) with children twice his size. He curses his mother at will, leaving her speechless. His temper is frightening to behold. One night when A-ki was trying to give him a bath, and he was trying to avoid it, he slapped her full in the face and said, "If you touch me, I'll have my father beat you to death." One afternoon he spent half an hour constructing a precarious pile of junk under our office window to provide a comfortable plat-form from which to observe us. His mother came by and ordered him down. Without even turning, he arrogantly told her, "Go away and don't bother me." There is an undefinable flair to his naughtiness that confuses his mother, makes his dour grandmother smile, and his fa-ther laugh outright. Even Lim Chieng-cua watches with amusement when this small boy, stick in hand, orders the whole lot of them off his playing field.

Lim Hue-lieng's youngest son, Masa, is the rebel of the family now, but unlike his father and his older brother there is no strong, compelling male personality in the family to bring his rebellion to a crisis. He hates the smothering life of the big family and the closed society of the village, and more than anything he hates the hard life of a farmer. He once told me that he thought his brother should not have married "because his wife has to work too hard." With complete seriousness he added, "If my girl saw all the work my brother's wife has to do, she would run away and never talk to me again." His earnest desire is to get a white-collar job that will take him out of the village forever, but his age is against him. Until he has completed the compulsory military training which he is still too young to begin, no one will hire him. So he lives in a limbo with the other young men his age, a limbo that seems designed to turn their young energy into trouble. He is the unquestioned leader of a large gang of young men, but instead of turning to the dubious activities of the lo *mua*, they are violent only in defending the good name of their district and chastis-ing in dark alleys any luckless mainland soldiers who force their attentions on "good" Taiwanese girls. Currently, their main activity seems to center on finding places to dance and people to dance with, an illegal activity during this period. Masa is much sought after as a dancing teacher and is reputed to be "the best." He is a romantically handsome boy with a surprising wave in his thick hair, but he does not look like a Lim. He has the charm, the temper, and the leadership potential typical of the rest of the Lims, but he is the only child of Lim Hue-lieng who has no physical resemblance to him. He has in-stead the short, square, powerful body of his mother, a rounder face and the broad Taiwanese nose.

I neglected to ask the family why he was known by a Japanese nickname, but regardless of the reason the name is appropriate. The image of Japan held by the younger people in the village is a com-posite of Japanese popular songs, colorful Japanese movies, and soft drink advertisements picturing pretty Japanese girls with friendly smiles. Masa is one of many village boys who cherish this image as an alternative to the life they know in Peihotien. As the men of his grandfather's generation chaffed under the restrictions of a Japanese colonial government and longed for the return of a Chinese adminis-tration that they could not remember, so the young men of today look upon a past they were too young to know, as a time of freedom and plenty. They read the second rate Japanese novels that are banned on Taiwan, and wear with excessive arrogance the humble Japanese zori that the Chinese government foolishly attempted to ban (and has since started manufacturing themselves). Nearly all of these young people have stop-gap jobs of one sort or another which bring them a little spending money but nothing that suggests a beginning in adult life. They simply wait, passing the time as pleasantly as they can. Masa and several others his age participate in the village band that marches in all religious processions, but the religion itself they scorn. Few Taiwanese take religion with the earnest seriousness that West-erners demand, but the young men of Masa's group (and that does not include all the young people of the village) laugh at the shamans, regard the priests in the temples as cynical men who have found a soft job, and ancestor worship as a tradition that must be carried on only for the pleasure it gives the old people in the family.

On the day I watched the annual fire-walking—an awesome ceremony
in which barefoot men in a state of possession carry the images of the
gods across a bed of hot coals—I saw Masa stop for a moment on his
way to Tapu to look at the proceedings. I asked him later if he
thought the gods had really entered the bearers' bodies and if not, why
they acted so strangely. He laughed at me and at the whole affair and
said the men looked to him like they were dancing "rock and roll"—for
all he knew, they were practicing their dance steps.

Instead of remonstrating with Masa over the rather frivolous life
he leads, A-pou and A-bok feel very sorry for him. Although A-bok
has some understanding of his uncle's problems, his mother does not,
and she assumes that if his uncle wanted, he could find a good paying
job for Masa that would provide him with the kind of future he
desires. Neither his mother nor his brother make any attempt to interest Masa in farming or confess to any hope that he will stay in the
village. They act as if he had no responsibility to the family and is
indeed only their pampered guest. His life and his grandfather's over-
lapped too briefly for the old man to leave his stamp. Masa resents his
uncle's management of the family, but instead of urging his brother to
divide the household, he rejects the whole system. The struggle within
the family is to him but one more indication of what is wrong with the
old ways.

⚜

chapter 8

TAN A-HONG: AN ADOPTED DAUGHTER

⚜

Except on the coldest days and for a few hours each night, the doors of the houses in Peihotien are never closed. A closed door in the daytime would arouse concern or suspicion and would surely bring a group of neighbors to inquire as to what the trouble might be. Few strangers come to Peihotien and when they do, they nearly always send one of the swarming children to run ahead and announce to Mr. Lim or Mr. Ong that he has a visitor. A neighbor looking for Mr. Lim or Mr. Ong simply walks into the house calling his name, and if Mr. Lim or Mr. Ong does not answer, he walks on out again. An intimate friend or relative walks into the house even more casually, wandering through the passageways until he finds someone, courteously cough-ing before pushing aside the curtains of a bedroom door in his search. Until I became familiar with the faces of the intimates of the Lim family and with the villagers who dropped in there frequently, I had the uncomfortable sensation that the narrow passageways of our house were thoroughfares at least as public as the lanes outside. The situation was even more confusing to me as a newcomer because the number of people actually living in the house varied from week to week. During the harvest season, gangs of workmen came up from the south to cut the rice and stayed in the house for the three or four days it took to harvest the Lim fields. When Lim A-bok strained his back, a young relative lived in the house and helped with the field work. At least twice an old woman distantly related through Lim Han-ci's wife stayed in the house for several weeks while the Lims tried to patch up her quarrel with her daughter. Other relatives came to stay for a few nights or a few months.

When Tan A·hong appeared with her five·year·old daughter, I had become so used to the stream of visitors that I didn't even bother to ask who she was for a week or so. I knew, of course, her surname, but when I casually asked A·bok's giddy wife if she was a relative, I dismissed the confused yes·and·no of her answer as just one more sample of A·ki's disorderly thoughts. However, as Tan A·hong's visit lengthened, we noticed that she consistently used kinship terms when addressing the Lims. She was visited frequently by an unusually at· tractive young woman who was introduced as her daughter and who was treated by the Lims as a much beloved family member. It did not take many questions to discover that Tan A·hong was the adopted daughter Lim Han·ci had given to another family when his own daughter was returned by her foster family. Tan A·hong remained in our house for several months and when one of the small village houses owned by the Lims became vacant, she moved into it, becom· ing a resident of Peihotien.

By Taiwanese standards, Lim Han·ci had been generous in his treatment of Tan A·hong. Since she was "only an adopted daughter," he would have been justified in selling her to the highest bidder when he found he no longer had reason to keep her and could no longer afford to keep her. The highest bidders in those days were dealers who bought attractive female children to raise as prostitutes, wealthy fami· lies who wanted slaves, or prostitutes who adopted daughters to raise in their profession as support for their own old age. Instead of this, Lim Han·ci arranged for A·hong's future in the way he would have arranged the future of a daughter born to him: he found a family who wished to adopt a girl as their son's future wife. A·hong was not sweet· tempered, even as a girl. The family who adopted her evidently had second thoughts about marrying her to their son. She was married out of the family. At least A·hong claims that her exit from the Tan family was by way of a respectable marriage, but the facts of her subsequent career and her retention of the Tan surname cast some doubt on this. The marriage, if it existed, was brief, for Tan A·hong soon moved to southern Taiwan where she earned her living as a prostitute. It was at this time that she further altered her name to include the character for phoenix (*hong*) which is often found in the professional names of women who follow her calling.

Legally and socially, the obligations of the Lims toward A·hong ceased when she entered the family of Tan. Even though she had been an adopted daughter in the Lim house for ten years, she had been sent with all propriety to the home of her future husband. If she left that family as a respectable bride, she should have brought her troubles back to them, or even to her natal family if she knew their whereabouts. Instead, A-hong always brought her problems home to the Lims. A quarrel with the man who was currently supporting her was grounds for a week's vacation at the Lim's. If she had trouble finding a new "friend," she stayed for awhile with the Lims. Her eldest daughter, Chun-ieng, spent as much of her childhood under the care of Lim Han-ci's wife and Lim A-pou as she did with her mother. Why Tan A-hong felt she could make such demands on the family, and why they allowed it, is a puzzle, but she continues to do so to this day.

Chun-ieng was born during the war. Many children were sent into the country during those years to protect them from the American bombings and so Chun-ieng, of course, was sent to the Lims. A-hong's second child was a son. When he was five or six, A-hong was living with a man, apparently not his father, in Tainan. They quarreled one evening and in a fit of temper she ran out, leaving him with the boy. She stayed away for nearly two weeks, during which time the boy contracted measles. A-hong's gentleman friend did his best at an unfamiliar job, but when A-hong recovered her good humor and returned, her son was dead. Sometime later she adopted a daughter who succumbed to a similar disease before she was old enough to walk. Finally, in A-hong's fortieth year, when her fading looks had forced her to work in the least desirable brothels of Tainan, she gave birth to her daughter, Chai-ngo.

When I met Tan A-hong, it was as hard to believe that she was only forty-five as it was to believe that she had once been a very pretty woman. She is quite short, fine boned, with delicate wrists and ankles, but now her back is stooped and her shoulders hunched, perhaps, as many people suggest, from the long hours she spends at the gambling tables. Her face is beautifully proportioned with a small, thin nose, high cheek bones, fairly large eyes and a fine wide brow. But now, her cheeks are sunken and lined, and her high cheek bones suggest too strongly the skeleton that lies beneath the sallow, muddy skin. Her hair is no longer thick, but it is still unusually fine in texture. She combs it so rarely that its quality goes unnoticed. She dresses in the fashion of the poorest village wife, sloppily and with not a few greasy spots on her skirt—but the sweater she throws over her shoulders is often imported. Her voice is shrill or gives that impression because she is nearly always scolding or complaining about something, but one can imagine that it was once a light feminine soprano.

Tan A-hong had not had any permanent "friends" for some time before Chai-ngo was born, and after her birth she found it more and more difficult to make a living. Chun-ieng was sent out to work. She was nineteen when I first met her and had been working as a prostitute for four years. To me she seemed more like a sophisticated American teenager than the timid giggling village girls her age. She was considerably less curious about us then were her contemporaries in the village, but far less hesitant about satisfying her curiosity. The village girls went into paroxysms of shyness if I asked them a question, but Chun-ieng howled at my accent and then good-humoredly tried to answer my questions. I rarely saw her interacting with anyone her own age in the village, but she joins the games of small children with an abandon and glee that would bring blushes of shame to the cheeks of her stodgy peers. The childish pleasure she finds in cooking, in feeding the family's dog, or in watching a newly hatched flock of ducks is both unaffected and pathetic. When she is in the village, Chun-ieng dresses soberly and wears little or no make-up, but she is undeniably different from the other girls her age. Her upright bearing, her poise in conversation, and even her smooth, pale skin are out of place in the muddy lanes and the coarse brick farmhouses. She is tall, unlike her mother, but her bones have the same delicacy. Her face is long and thin, giving her high cheekbones the drama that her mother's lack. Her eyes are a bit too small, but she shapes her eyebrows carefully to minimize the defect. She doesn't cut her fine black hair, nor allow it to be frizzed by cheap permanents. Often in the village she pulls it back into a pony tail, giving her an innocent Alice-in-Wonderland look. She loves to gossip and has great skill in spinning a simple anecdote into an intriguing story. Without slipping into vulgarity, she can entertain the rather staid women of the Lim household with endless stories about her work—she can even keep Lim A-pou sitting for awhile. There is always more laughter in the house when Chun-ieng is home.

Prostitutes in Peihotien occupy a rather ambiguous position, resembling in no way the status forced on a prostitute, retired or active, in an American small town. They are considered "more inter-

esting" than other women of their age and income, but judgments
about their morality or respectability are not based on their profession. Too many village girls have had to "go out to work" to support
aging parents or young siblings. In recent years, there has only been
one girl in the area who entered a brothel by choice, lured by the fine
clothes and exciting life. More commonly, women become prostitutes
because they were raised for that purpose, or because their family is
desperately in need of the income. The villagers are not inclined to
think of these girls as martyrs since Chinese children are expected to
make great sacrifices for their parents, but they are not likely to
criticize them either. On the contrary, most villagers assume a girl has
amply repaid the debt she owes her parents for raising her when she
obeys their command to become a prostitute—repaid it more fully
than the daughter who remains at home can ever hope to. Parents can
nearly always count on the support of village opinion in deciding the
future of their daughter unless that daughter has supported the family
for several years by prostitution. By giving up her youth, the young
prostitute has gained a certain amount of control over her future. In
the village her respectability depends upon how careful she is to walk
within the paths of traditional morality when she is home for a few
days each month, how compliant she is in turning over the majority of
her earnings to her parents, and how cautious she is with village
males. A prostitute who carries on professional activities within the
village is in deep trouble. If her relatives are not aware of her indiscretion, they will be told, and that is usually enough. It is a small
community.

No one in the Lim family tried to conceal from us Tan A-hong's
former occupation or the source of Chun-ieng's present earnings.
They are not callous about Chun-ieng's fate, but they also see her soft
fingers resting next to their scarred, calloused hands, her delicate silk
dresses hanging beside their coarse, shapeless working clothes, her
closed bedroom door when they come in after three hours of early
morning weeding in the fields. About her future they feel pity, but the
life of a woman in a farm family is not easy either. In Chun-ieng's
difficulties with her mother, however, she has the family's complete
sympathy. They may chide her occasionally, or remind her of her
mother's seniority, but their words lack conviction. Tan A-hong's
outrageous behavior toward her daughter would challenge the beliefs
of the most adamant proponent of filial piety. In all fairness, I must

admit at this point to a strong prejudice against Tan A-hong. I could find in her no redeeming qualities. Her life has been hard and full of frustrations, but it was a way of life she chose in preference to that of marriage. She did not allow her daughter that choice.

Tan A-hong's latest return to Peihotien was primarily at her daughter's urging. To bring her mother north, Chun-ieng gave up a good, secure income in one of the best houses in Tainan and complicated a personal love affair that mattered a great deal to her. Her motives need little explanation: A-hong, as with many women her age and, in particular, women who have been prostitutes, is a habitual gambler. She gambles as long as she can find money and players. When she runs out of money, she sells anything at hand, borrows from anyone foolish enough to loan, and begs from those who refuse loans. Chun-ieng's beauty and vivacious personality provided her with a very good income, but her mother was spending the majority of it in the expensive twenty-four-hour gambling houses of Tainan. Chun-ieng had trouble meeting ordinary living expenses. So, she persuaded her mother to sell her small house, invested as much of the money as she could get away from her into gold (the landless person's only insurance against inflation), and moved her to Peihotien. While Chun-ieng went on to Taipei to find work, her mother searched out the small gambling dens of Hotien.

Their status as guests in the Lim house had no effect on the quarrels between A-hong and Chun-ieng. They were loud and bitter. One night when Chun-ieng returned from Taipei after an absence of a week, she was greeted with the news that her mother had lost over NT$700 in two nights of gambling—nearly a week's income for Chun-ieng and almost a month's income for the average family. Chun-ieng tactlessly demanded that her mother turn over the remainder of the money she had received from the sale of the house. A-hong, of course, refused. "This is my money. Why should I give it to you? Sure, I gamble, but what about you? Don't you ever gamble? You say you want to buy gold with it! Huh! You just want to spend it. You have your own money if you want to buy gold, and you already have plenty of gold hidden away, too. I want to keep my money. Maybe I'll buy some gold, too."

Chun-ieng answered her wearily, "All right, I'm not going to argue with you. I'm too tired. I just wanted to say something about it so that people would know I tried and would not blame me."

Although A-hong expects her daughter to provide for her as for a child, she resents being treated as a child. Chun-ieng's words angered her. "How can you be so shameless. I know what you are telling people—you are telling them I lost lots of money in Tainan and then sold your clothes and your gold to get more. You are shameless. You know how little money you gave me. You didn't give me all the money you earned so I had to take it. Aren't you ashamed to tell all those lies?"

This touched a sore spot in Chun-ieng. She wants very much to be considered a proper filial daughter and her mother accused her of withholding her earnings, a most unfilial act. Chun-ieng answered defensively, "There was nothing I could do. You are too fond of gambling. I can't turn all of the money over to you."

A-hong knows her adversary well. She decided to take advantage of the wound she had inflicted by putting a few more things before the public. (Most quarrels in China take place by preference before an audience and the attention of the combatants is directed as much to the effect of their words on the observers as upon each other.) With lip-curling malice, A-hong continued, "Ah, you are right. I like to gamble. And what is my dutiful daughter going to do about it? You, of course, never gamble, do you? You don't remember the time in Tainan when you lost all of the money you had earned for two days, and I had to come and tell you not to gamble any more? Do you remember what you said to your mother that day? You said you didn't care. You told me you could just go with any of the guests when you had no more money. You told your mother that you had no reason to save money and that there were women as old as me working there."

Chun-ieng looked tired and depressed. When she didn't answer, her mother tried to goad her into a response. "Well, I'm old now, I don't care if people laugh at me, but if you keep saying all those things, you know who people will be laughing at. At a shameless daughter!"

Chun-ieng got up to leave the room, but at the door she paused long enough to say, "You speak as though I enjoyed working in that place. Is that why you wouldn't let me come home, even when I begged?"

A few days later another argument on the same subject ended with A-hong threatening her daughter with a cleaver. Chun-ieng with a sincerity that frightened all of us, stood her ground and encouraged her mother. "Kill me. I truly don't care. Just kill me and be done with it." Lim A-pou pushed the girl out of the room.

Tan A-hong often accuses the Lims of conspiring with and pampering her daughter. Her accusations are not unjustified. The Lims keep Chun-ieng's secrets, hide her money, and even find time in their busy schedule to do her laundry when she is in the village. One day when the women were washing clothes at the river, I overheard the following exchange between A-bok's wife, A-ki, Iu Mui-mue (another adopted daughter of the Lim family), and a neighbor.

The neighbor asked, "Isn't that Chun-ieng's blouse?" A-ki nodded. The next question was inevitable. "Does she pay you for that?"

A-ki answered diffidently, "No, I only wash a few things for her when she is here."

Iu Mui-mue laughed and said, jealously, "She doesn't pay you, but she bought your baby an outfit that cost over a hundred dollars."

A-ki giggled and said, "That is why we say we are going to give her my daughter to be her adopted daughter."

Mui-mue responded, scornfully amused, "Adopted daughter! Yes, you'll give her to Chun-ieng now, but when she gets older, you'll want her back."

A-ki, still giggling, said, "That's just what Chun-ieng said the other day. She said, 'Oh, I'll adopt you now, little girl, and feed you, and when you get old enough to earn some money, you will give it all to your mother and not to me. No sense feeding you!' I told her she was the same way. Mother [A-pou] fed her when she was little, but now when she makes money, she gives it all to her own mother."

Mui-mue retorted, "She gives money to Lim A-pou, too."

A-ki was quite indignant. "She only gives her a few dollars now and then—nothing like she gives her mother."

Mui-mue countered that easily. "Well, A-hong has nobody to eat with [no family], so of course she has to give her more money."

A-ki began to worry that she had said too much. "Chun-ieng treats her mother very well. She buys her the best food and lots of nice clothes and gives her money to gamble with. She treats her very well."

The neighbor, one of A-hong s gambling companions, disagreed.

"Hah! How good is that. I always hear her scolding her mother. She tries to restrain her at every turn."

A-ki bristled in defense of her friend. "That is because the mother doesn't have any sense. If her mother took care of the home and didn't gamble all the time, I'm sure Chun-ieng would give her all of the money to take care of."

The continuous quarrel between A-hong and her daughter over money reached a climax several months later. It was only then that I learned of the future Chun-ieng longed for and of the secret she and the Lim family had kept from her mother. While working in Tainan, Chun-ieng met the second son of a wealthy industrialist. Their mutual attraction deepened into a more serious interest, and the young man wanted to marry her. Many young prostitutes who have not yet compromised their future by a series of abortions, illegitimate children, or the adoption of young girls as support for their old age, marry into quite respectable families. There seems to be some notion among peasant families that a young woman who has had this kind of experience is less likely to succumb to temptation after marriage. Chun-ieng's young man, however, came from the upper classes and her welcome into his family might not be as warm. Moreover, they also had to wait until his older brother, then serving his term in the army, was married, it being bad form for a younger brother to marry before an elder. When Chun-ieng's lover was sent by his father to supervise a logging operation in central Taiwan, they decided upon a compromise. Chun-ieng would come and live with him there until such time as they could be married properly. Tan A-hong knew nothing of these plans, although she knew her daughter was fond of the young man. She herself was attracted by his reputed wealth, but the possibility of her daughter marrying anyone was something she refused to think about. Chun-ieng married would not only make a considerable dent in A-hong's income, but would also deprive her of her authority over the girl. No matter what agreements are reached at the time of marriage, a young woman's loyalty necessarily shifts to her husband. Besides, Chun-ieng was still approaching the peak of her earning power as a prostitute. Her youth and high spirits had brought her a good income until now, and A-hong's practiced eyes recognized that her daughter's appeal was based on a handsomeness that would not fade as had her own but might with training turn Chun-ieng into the cool, sophisticated companion of the very wealthy. Whether or not Chun-ieng's talents are up to her mother's ambitions is hard to say, but with this possibility in mind, A-hong was not likely to smile upon a promise of marriage, even from the son of a wealthy industrialist.

I never found out how Tan A-hong discovered the young people's plans, but it was probably through an intercepted letter. After telling the Lim family about her daughter's deceit, A-hong set out for Taipei to confront Chun-ieng in the wine house where she worked. Lim A-pou, fearing a serious outcome, accompanied her. When mother and daughter met, there was a violent scene. Chun-ieng tried to explain that she had been putting gold away for her mother's support and that she and her lover planned to send her a generous allowance, but A-hong was too angry, and perhaps too frightened, to pay any attention. She slapped Chun-ieng repeatedly, accused her of vile deeds, and told her to "go die." Chun-ieng ran out of the room, promising her mother that she would kill herself at once. Lim A-pou, who must have seemed wildly incongruous in this setting, sent A-hong away and searched the building for Chun-ieng. The girl was not to be found, so A-pou rushed back to the village to consult with Lim Chieng-cua. A young woman's threat of suicide is not taken lightly on Taiwan—their alternatives are too few. As soon as he heard A-pou's description of the encounter, Lim Chieng-cua hurried to Tapu where he phoned relatives and friends in Taipei to organize a search.

Thus began a long tense afternoon of waiting. Tan A-hong sat in A-pou's bedroom, her mood varying between remorse and fury at the "thankless girl." In the midst of this anxious suspense, Li Guat-ngo, Lim A-pou's adopted daughter and Chun-ieng's childhood playmate, arrived to pay a visit to her family and in particular to Chun-ieng. Li Guat-ngo is now the wife of a moderately prosperous shopkeeper; she has two children, good humor, and a tendency to speak her mind.

She listened with concern to her foster mother's account of the morning's events, casting looks of utter disgust at Tan A-hong. When A-hong began a tirade of complaints against Chun-ieng, Guat-ngo refused to listen. "Do you want her to die? What if she does kill herself? What will you do then? She has been very good to you. You must have a very bad heart to talk this way."

Angered, Tan A-hong answered, "I have a bad heart? You wait until your children get older and treat you like she treats me. Then you'll know what I'm talking about."

Guat-ngo: "If my daughter is like her, I will consider myself very fortunate. Don't be so black-hearted. She is twenty years old now. If she wants to get married, she can do it, and you can't do anything about it. You can't get any more money from her then, can you?"

A-hong: "That's good! Let her just try and run away from me. Get married? Let her try! If she is going to die, it is going to be in one of two ways—either she'll die on the road [i.e. homeless, friendless, impoverished] or she'll die by my hand!"

Guat-ngo was shocked. She stared at the older woman, speechless. Finally, she said, "You are not a mother at all. You never fed her. That must be why you can say these terrible things. Now she earns lots of money for you to gamble and eat and buy pretty clothes. Isn't that enough? You had better think that's enough."

A-hong: "That's right! I never fed her, indeed! It was war-time then and I had to search all over to find powdered milk for her, and when I found it, I had to pay to mail it all the way home here. I was going to hire someone to take care of her, but A-pou's mother wanted her so I sent her home. And how do you know she gives me so much money? Are you her go-between? What do you know about it? What do you know about anything?"

By this time, A-hong was shrieking. Her shrill voice could be heard all over the house. "I'm well over forty years old. I don't have her by my side, but I'm still alive. I'm not freezing or starving. I want her to die on the road! I want her to die by my hands! I want her to die." A-hong added as an afterthought—the afterthought that so often makes Taiwanese women's quarrels so ludicrous: "I can get a job as a cook for someone."

Guat-ngo was not to be silenced by histrionics. She returned to her scolding. "Yes, you sent a lot of powdered milk home for your daughter! Why was it then that poor grandmother was up late every night grinding rice to make gruel for her? You never fed her. She had no milk to drink. No wonder you don't care if she dies."

A-hong: "You were just a child. What do you know about it? You say I never took care of her. She is over twenty years old and in all of that time I never took care of her? You don't know anything about it. All the people in this family side with her. They always say she is right. That is why she treats me so badly now. They let her do whatever she wanted to do."

Lim A-pou had been keeping out of the argument and trying by hand signals to get her daughter to drop it. When Tan A-hong began to criticize the family, however, she looked very stern and said, "Be careful of your words. My mother and father treated her like a grand-child. They are dead now, but I am not. You never thanked them for taking care of her for you, and you had better not criticize them either."

Guat-ngo: "And what do you mean I don't know anything about it? I was nine years old when she came here, and I often carried her on my back. When she was little she often fainted, and she often had convulsions. Did *you* know that? Did *you* ever take care of her when she was sick?"

Lim A-pou recovered her calm face, but was still stern looking. "Your daughter is your daughter," she said. "No matter how bad, she is still your daughter, and no matter how bad you are, you are still her mother. You must not keep saying you want her to die. She buys nice things to feed you and nice clothes for you to wear, and she does this only for you. You are the only one she gives things to, except the children now and then. If you want to treat her badly, we cannot stop you, but because I took care of her when she was little, I have a right to say some things. If you want to be someone's servant, you won't find it such a bad job. Anybody can be a servant. You had better take a look at yourself first, though. Are you healthy enough for that?" Tan A-hong suffers from asthma and is extremely thin, both conditions exacerbated by her all night gambling and chain smoking.

A-hong: "My bad health is her fault, too. When my youngest daughter was born, it was winter and Chun-ieng refused to wash or cook for me so I had to get up and do it myself. My bad health is all due to her. She refused to help me. I want her to die. If she won't treat me like a mother, I won't treat her like a daughter."

Guat-ngo: "You just think it over. There may be some daughters who treat their mothers better than Chun-ieng treats you, but if my daughter treats me as well, I will say that I have great good for-tune."

A-pou: "Your lot in life compares better with rich people than with mine. I have two sons, but even sons can't buy clothes for me. You only have a daughter, but look what a pretty sweater she bought you."

A-hong threw the sweater on the floor and said, "Pretty sweater! I may be over forty, but I don't need that wretch to feed me. She never has fed me."

Guat-ngo laughed at the absurdity of this statement. "If she has never fed you, where do you get all the money to eat? If she never gives you any money, where do you get all the money for this?" She made gambling motions with her hands. "Just where do you get your pretty clothes and fine white rice?"

Tan A-hong grew hysterical and began screaming curses at the younger woman, threatening to hit her. A-pou made her daughter leave the room. This calmed A-hong somewhat, but she continued her complaints and again began to accuse the Lims, in particular Lim Han-ci and his wife, of teaching her daughter to disobey her.

Lim Chieng-cua, who had returned from Tapu part way through the quarrel, was sitting in the next room, trying to ignore the angry voices. When A-hong spoke of his parents, he stalked into the bed-room and, very red in the face, demanded, "Has anyone asked you for money in all the time you have lived here and eaten here? Nobody wants to hear your noise. You are not right, but you think you are very smart. I have scolded your daughter several times for not being more polite to you, even though I knew she was in the right and you deserved whatever harsh words she gave you. There are several peo-ple here who are not relatives who can tell you that this is true. It is only a mother who can decide whether a girl is good or bad, but I want you to listen to this. She is not as bad as you are trying to make people believe."

Lim Chieng-cua's anger subsided when A-hong began to cry. He continued scolding her, however, sounding very much like a school-master reading lessons. "I have heard mothers say that they wanted their daughters to die, but I have never heard a real mother say this. It was always a foster mother or a stepmother. Why is it that you talk this way? You think it over for awhile. You tell us she only left you a few dollars for the whole week. You never tell her the truth, so she never knows whether you really need money or not. If you really need money you can just tell her how much you need and she will give it to you. Why must you keep pushing the girl all the time? You are her mother. She knows she has to take care of you."

A-hong, sobbing, said, "You didn't see her yesterday. You don't know what her face looks like when I ask her for money."

"I do know," Lim Chieng-cua rejoined. "I have seen that expres-sion, and it is one of the things I have scolded her about. But, if you never lied to her, if you always treated her like your own daughter and not an adopted daughter, she wouldn't be that way. She doesn't know whether you really need money or not. You have lost every dollar you got from selling your house now. Sure, that was your own money to do with as you wished, but you think about that, too. She is getting older and she is going to take care of you after she's married, but she won't be able to give you so much money to gamble with. Married or not, she won't be able to make this much money in a few more years. If you had another NT$10,000 to gamble with, you wouldn't be in this mood today."

As he left the room, Lim Chieng-cua added: "It is a rule that a child *must* be good to his parents, but parents have to treat their children decently, too. That is also a rule. You can do many things to your children, but there is a point beyond which you cannot go. You have already gone too far. You must stop pushing her. If she is dead, your next daughter is too young to be of any use to you. What will you do?"

Tan A-hong, crying quietly, went home.

Late that evening, Lim Chieng-cua was summoned to Tapu to receive a telephone call. One of the children was sent to tell A-hong. She was a pitiful sight as she walked into the house. Her anger was gone and her terror reduced her to listing absurd reasons as to why Chun-ieng would not kill herself. When Lim Chieng-cua returned, he told the assembled group that Chun-ieng had been found and was in good health. He didn't even look at Tan A-hong and retired at once to his bedroom.

Chun-ieng returned to Peihotien late the next day, and I'm afraid the villagers were rather disappointed by her appearance. She should have looked wan and dejected, but instead she looked happier than I have ever seen her. She amiably satisfied the curiosity of her neighbors, saving the details of her adventure for the family. Her skill in story-telling did not suffer even when the story was at her own expense. After running out of the wine house, she bought some poison and went to a hotel. She gave us a humorous description of the delighted, if bewildered, pedi-cab driver to whom she gave the last of her money. Just as she was about to take the pills, she heard someone in the hotel being called to the telephone and decided she should phone her lover in Tainan so that he wouldn't think she had killed herself because of something he had done. The connection was, of course, bad, so the boyfriend made her promise to wait until he could get to Taipei to talk with her. She then spent an entertaining hour trying to locate some relatives who would come and pay her hotel bill.

The source of Chun-ieng's unexpected happiness was revealed more slowly. Tan A-hong's complaints about her daughter were not completely groundless. Chun-ieng often answered her angry words with scorn and disrespect. She did not trust her mother and sometimes treated her honest need for money with disdain—understandable per- haps, but not behavior expected of a dutiful daughter. Unfortunately, Chun-ieng *was* a dutiful daughter. The anguish which prompted her toward suicide was as much the result of her own self-blame as of her mother's imprecations. Lim A-pou told me many months later that this was not the first time Chun-ieng had contemplated leaving her mother (always with adequate financial provision), but each time she had felt sorry for the older woman and returned. The interview that took place with her lover when he arrived from Tainan seemed to provide another solution. He generously proposed that she give up her plan of joining him, but also give up her work in the winehouse. He would send her a weekly allowance (the sum of which caused many round eyes) and visit her as often as possible until the day when they could be married. After their marriage, they would decide what to do about her mother. This was indeed a fairy-tale ending if it had been in fact the ending.

We had the pleasure of Chun-ieng's presence around the village for several months. Her boyfriend visited fairly regularly and she occasionally went to see him. Needless to say, each of her trips was preceded by anxious ill-temper on the part of Tan A-hong, but Chun- ieng always returned at the appointed time. Their quarrels were either less frequent or less violent because they came to my attention only rarely during those months. After awhile, though, I began to see more of Chun-ieng in the Lim house, often in tears, and I heard more of Tan A-hong's gambling debts. It wasn't long before Chun-ieng started disappearing from the village for two or three days at a time. I asked the family about her absences and received noncommittal answers until finally Lim A-pou admitted that she had returned to work. When I asked what would happen if her boyfriend unexpectedly turned up, Lim A-pou told me sadly, "We are supposed to tell him she has gone to work as a hostess in a coffee shop and we don't know where it is." Whether her lover discovered her deception or whether Chun-ieng herself finally gave up hope, I never found out, but after a few more months his visits to the village ceased, and Chun-ieng spent most of her time in Taipei. The Lims had little to say on the subject, but I don't think I only imagined that Tan A-hong came to the house considerably less often than was her wont. Perhaps she was just busier at her gambling.

During the last few months of my stay with the Lims, I noticed Lim A-pou make several trips out of the village dressed in her formal dark clothing. I asked A-ki where her mother-in-law was going, but got only a sad shake of the head. Then one day Lim A-pou returned with Chun-ieng, accompanied by a pretty though very frightened four-year-old girl. At Chun-ieng's request, Lim A-pou had found her a daughter to adopt. Chun-ieng stayed home from work for several days, spending all her time with the child, trying to coax a smile or a few words from her frightened lips. She played games with her, told her stories, bought her candy, and changed her clothes half a dozen times a day. Before Chun-ieng returned to work, the glazed look in her foster daughter's eyes was gone, but she looked terrified whenever Chun-ieng left the room. When Chun-ieng returned to Taipei, this second abandonment seemed too great for her daughter to bear. Day after day the child sat in the guest hall, her tiny body pulled up to occupy the smallest amount of space in the wicker chair, her eyes dully resting on the floor. The busy adults tried to lure her into activity and even the children treated her with special consideration, but nothing seemed to have any effect. When ordered to eat, she ate, but as soon as possible she would crawl back into the chair. She never cried and as far as I know never spoke. Her grief totally engulfed her. I am still haunted by that tiny figure of silent despair crouching in the shadows of the empty guest hall. Her despair was to me, and from their sad faces, to the Lims as well, a symbol of Chun-ieng's despair. Chun-ieng had at last accepted her mother's profession and turned her back on dreams of a normal life.

chapter 9

IU MUI-MUE:
A
REJECTED
BRIDE

By the time Lim Chieng-cua and Iu Mui-mue, the girl adopted to be his wife, reached marriageable age, the Lim family was prosperous— more prosperous than their neighbors and more prosperous than Lim Han-ci had ever dreamed of their being within his lifetime. Iu Mui-mue had been adopted to provide a dutiful daughter-in-law and an inexpensive wife for the second son of a respectable though poor tenant farm family. But, the poor tenant family had become an increasingly powerful landed family, a family that could now afford a more prestigious form of marriage. Even if there had not been a change in his fortunes, Lim Han-ci could see that Mui-mue was not a suitable wife for his son. By adopting her as a child he had avoided the problem of adjusting an adult bride to a new household, but there are some things adopting parents cannot control. In the case of Mui-mue, it was her stupidity. Even worse, for Lim Han-ci's temperament, she was feckless. In all of his other children and in those of his grandchildren old enough to be influenced by him, Lim Han-ci instilled a driving capacity for hard work, but Mui-mue turned out to be one of the laziest women in Peihotien. She is placid, shiftless, and pleasure loving; when she encounters a problem, she laughs and turns to something else. In her youth she got more personal enjoyment out of the Lims' new prosperity than any other family member. By the time she was eighteen, she had a surprising reputation (for those days) for looseness, a reputation that Lim Han-ci found he could not cure by beating. Lim Chieng-cua at twenty-one had already developed some skills in diplomacy. When he committed his only unfilial act, refusing to marry the girl selected for him by his parents, he did so in terms of her potential for bringing shame to the family name.

Several young men of Lim Chieng-cua's generation rejected the girls adopted to be their brides, but it was by no means the common act it was to become a few years later. In most cases there was a family uproar, aired from one end of the village to the other; the outcome depended a great deal upon the son's position in the family, the firmness of his character, and the potential he had for financial independence. In the case of the Lims, however, the village knew nothing of the matter until an observant neighbor noted the second visit of a go-between and was calmly told that Lim Han-ci was arrang-ing the marriage of his adopted daughter. We can never know pre-cisely what words were exchanged between father and son, but I doubt that they found much to disagree over. Lim Han-ci could not have looked with much favor on Iu Mui-mue, and he certainly real-ized that her nature would not improve with an elevation of position in the family. Had the old man wanted it, Lim Chieng-cua would probably be married to Mui-mue today, but since the father was in basic agreement with his son, there was no reason for him to rise to the challenge to his authority and to thereby endanger a relationship that was both comforting and important to his own well-being. Lim Han-ci had lost his eldest son and wished no quarrel with his one remaining son.

There is nothing in the marriage of adopted siblings that is lack-ing in honor. It is a form of marriage found even among wealthy urban families who value peace over pageantry. But even a man of Lim Han-ci's parsimonious principles must have been tempted by the opportunity the marriage of two unrelated adults provides for a public display of the family's rise in the world. To affirm his ability to provide a series of feasts for a hundred or more guests, to display his new house bedecked in satin banners and garlands of gift money, to introduce the quantity and quality of his social and blood relations, to show how large a dowry he could demand, to have the dowry carried on open carts through the streets of the town and the paths of the villages, to know that rumors were circulating as to the amount he gave as a "bride price"—these things may have appealed to Lim Han-ci as a symbol of his personal triumph over poverty and as a gesture of gratitude to the son who had remained loyal to him. A poor family with no money and no land can marry a son to a foster daughter and their neighbors will think nothing of it; when a family as affluent as Lim Han-ci's makes such a marriage, it only reminds the neighbors of how insignificant that family was when the bride was adopted. The Lim family had climbed to a definite social position in their community and Lim Han-ci was willing to pay the price to maintain it.

Mui-mue's character and limited intellectual capacities cast doubt on her ability to function as the wife of the family's head. With the removal of his eldest son from an active role in family affairs, Lim Han-ci departed from custom and began to look to his second son as his natural successor. So long as he lived, Lim Han-ci retained and made the most of his authority as father, but he gradually turned over to Lim Chieng-cua the practical conduct of the family's affairs. Lim Han-ci continued to represent the family in the village and to conduct most of its external affairs, but more and more decisions about the use of family funds, the purchase of supplies, the keeping of family accounts, were delegated to Chieng-cua. As Chieng-cua's wife, Mui-mue would be expected to eventually assume management of the family's domestic affairs, and this was a task for which she had again and again demonstrated herself as unfit. By now the family was convinced that Mui-mue could not be trusted with access to their common purse. Lim A-pou would have been the ideal woman to fill this role, but that was impossible. The only solution was to remove Mui-mue and find another wife for Lim Chieng-cua.

From what I heard of her early personality and from what I can infer from her present behavior, the marriage Lim Han-ci negotiated for Iu Mui-mue seemed quite appropriate. Through the good offices of a go-between, she was quietly and respectably married to a medicine peddler from a nearby town. Medicine peddlers are rarely wealthy and usually spend a great deal of time traveling, but their life is full of variety and in general freer than that in the villages. This nomadic existence with its constant stimulation should have been ideal for Mui-mue, but for some reason it was not. Perhaps instead of traveling with her husband, she was left at home with his parents, or perhaps her easy ways and lack of judgment got her into trouble. Whatever the cause, the marriage lasted for a very short period, less than a year. I have reason to believe that the failure of the marriage rested on her actions since had it been otherwise, she would have returned to the

Lim home from which she was properly married and let them take responsibility for smoothing out the difficulties—a form of behavior in which Mui-mue was well practiced. Instead, Iu Mui-mue resumed the name of her natal family, although she did not revive any other relations with them, and moved to the city of Keelung. Keelung is a port city and the brothels there are not the prosperous, gay sin spots frequented by Tan A-hong and her daughter, Chun-ieng. Even in her youth Iu Mui-mue couldn't have been attractive enough to find employment in a better class house, and her lethargy and lack of intelligence would not have allowed her to try any other form of employment. Nonetheless, her good humor alone seems to have provided her with enough "friends" to support herself. She returned to the Lim household infrequently.

Much to the disgust of some of our informants, the most scornful of whom had herself worked for several years as a prostitute, Mui-mue contracted syphilis. To be specific, the disgust of her acquaintances was engendered not so much by the fact that she contracted the disease, an obvious occupational hazard, but by the fact that she neglected it until her legs were a mass of loathesome sores. Someone finally forced medical attention on her and she was cured, but her legs are deeply scarred.

Iu Mui-mue was twenty-eight when her first child, a girl, was born. Her chronology is a bit hazy here since it was also at about this time that she began living with a gardener. After a few years she and the gardener were married. That is, they registered their names jointly with the police. Shortly after attaining this respectable status, Mui-mue succumbed to the attraction of the house of Lim and returned to Peihotien. She and her husband now rent another of the little houses owned by the Lims. She is in and out of the main house somewhat more than other neighbors, always helps in the kitchen when the family gives a big feast, is usually the first asked when A-bok must hire a woman to weed or clean vegetables. There is considerable reticence about discussing family affairs in her presence as she is no more capable of keeping a secret than she is capable of tact. In the family schism, she is notoriously prejudiced toward Lim A-pou's point of view and when lacking evidence for her case does not hesitate to manufacture it.

Iu Mui-mue's marriage seems as stable and as happy as any of the other relationships in Peihotien, both formal and informal. Her

husband is considerably older than she, which is not particularly unusual, and he seems blessed with no more sense or responsibility than
his wife. He has worked in the gardens of American military and
embassy families on occasion, but now that the early days of gross
overpayment are finished, he is resentful of the wages he is paid (usually about twice what any Chinese would consider paying). He never
has a steady job and makes little effort in that direction, but when he
does find something that pays well, the family lives high. I overheard
the following conversation between Lim Chui-ieng and Tan A-hong
about their mutual relative when they found out that Mui-mue's husband had found a profitable job.

A-hong: "He has already made over NT$3,000 and now they
have set him to planting trees at the flour mill in Tapu. He is getting
paid ten dollars a tree! But, neither of them think of paying back the
money they owe. They just buy new clothes, and more food than a
family twice their size could eat, and Mui-mue gambles every day."

Lim Chui-ieng: "I never could do the way she does. She only
thinks about borrowing the money and never about the next time she
may need to borrow. Every time you ask them to pay you back, they
say they will pay you as soon as they get some money. It's only her
mouth that says this though, it never gets into her head."

A-hong: "That's right. We always worry when we owe people
money, but those two! The husband and wife are just the same! A-bok
has seen him come home several times with a big basket of peaches. I
would never dare buy peaches."

Lim Chui-ieng: "My children don't even know what a peach
tastes like."

A-hong: "Mui-mue doesn't understand anything at all about *cue
lang* [obligations to people]. Like that time when her son was so sick
and they didn't have enough money to take the child to a doctor. My
daughter gave her some rings to pawn, but instead she took them
around to different people and borrowed money from them all. When
Chun-ieng found out about it, she had to go around and pay all the
people. Mui-mue never did pay Chun-ieng the money. If she under-
stood about *cue lang,* she would always be grateful to my Chun-ieng
because her child would be dead now if it weren't for her. Instead, she
doesn't even pay her back the money."

The two women continued discussing Iu Mui-mue's various strat-
egies for obtaining money, Lim Chui-ieng admitting that even she had

made the mistake once of borrowing money for her which she finally had to repay herself. Tan A-hong who lives next door to Mui-mue said that someone or other comes nearly every day to try to get money owed to them. The two women then tried to calculate the debts known to them and came up with a figure close to NT$10,000, not including their current bill at Ng's store. Tan A-hong's righteous indignation at Mui-mue's debts and daily gambling may strike the reader as hypo-critical, but in a village economy Mui-mue's peccadilloes are less forgivable than A-hong's. The latter pays her debts, albeit with her daughter's money, but Mui-mue borrows from non-relatives as from relatives with no serious plan for repayment. The long suffering wife of the village storekeeper told me one day, "That Iu Mui-mue! Her body is stuffed with borrowed money! She has charged over NT$800 worth of rice from me alone. You don't even have to talk about all the other food. She borrowed over NT$400 from my father-in-law a long time ago. Every time I ask her to pay some of her bill, she says she doesn't have any money, but then she is always off somewhere gam-bling. She never stops to think 'I owe lots of people money. I should stop gambling.' "

Iu Mui-mue and her husband are both gamblers but on a modest scale. They have neither enough money nor wits to spend the long hours at the tables with the real addicts. Mui-mue provides the serious gamblers with great amusement because of her children. The girl is old enough now to run herd on the two smaller boys, but when their mother is gambling, all three frequently gang up on the poor woman and create terrible scenes until she bribes them outdoors with money for candy and cookies. Since she usually enters the games with small capital, the children cut her playing time to a minimum. Her own voracious appetite consumes what little she may win.

I have often wondered what it was that attracted Mui-mue's husband and what it is that keeps him with her. Physically, she couldn't have been very appealing when they met, and she certainly hasn't improved since. She is fat, not in the sleek, shining manner of a prosperous Chinese matron, but with the lumpy, coarseness of a slat-tern in any culture. Her abilities as a housewife are minimal and her meals haphazard. Although her eldest child is a pleasant, patient girl and is perhaps a bit more intelligent than the rest of the family, she is growing sneaky and spiteful with the burden of the two little boys constantly on her hands. The boys are literally borderline cases. The eldest is aptly nicknamed "Dumby" by the village children. When I left the village, he was becoming quite vicious as a result of the cruel teasing of his peers. His sister does her best to protect him, but Iu Mui-mue, except for an occasional shout at his persecutors, seems unconcerned. The father is not particularly well received in the village, probably because of his and his wife's capacity for accumulating hopeless debts. I never saw him at a feast in the Lim house, even when his wife was helping in the kitchen. Yet, between husband and wife there seems to be a steady, stable affection. Few marital disputes are missed by the village gossips, but I rarely heard of a disturbance in their household. The only long-standing disagreement they have, one which would have been major in other families, is about the terms of their marriage. Mui-mue's husband claims that his wife married into his line of descent, but his wife claims that he married into hers. As evidence for her case, Mui-mue points out that the eldest child carries her family surname. Her husband claims that this is simply an error in registration that he will have changed. The "error in registration" may very well have occurred before Mui-mue and her husband were married. During my stay in the village, the registration was never changed, the disagreement never resolved, and the debts never paid.

Before their marriage there is rarely anything in the behavior of betrothed foster siblings that distinguishes them from true brothers and sisters. The present relationship between Lim Chieng-cua and Mui-mue is probably somewhat more distant than is usual between a man and his married sister, but considering the two personalities involved, and their present, very different, statuses, this is not too surprising. Iu Mui-mue is certainly not secretive about her sympathy with Lim A-pou in the current family disagreement, but sisters are nearly always closer to each other than they are to their brothers. Mui-mue is not given to reflection, but any opinion or thought that does occur to her is usually expressed loudly to anyone who will listen. If she ever stopped to consider how close she came to occupying Lim Chui-ieng's comfortable position rather than her own precarious one, she has long since forgotten about it. Mui-mue is clearly a victim of the Lim family's change of fortune, but in fact I think she is quite content with her life.

chapter 10

LIM CHUI-IENG:
AN
EXPENSIVE
WIFE

Lim Chieng-cua's revolt, it if may be called that, ended with his refusal to marry Iu Mui-mue. He did not demand the right to choose his own bride and made no objection when his father began searching about for a trustworthy go-between. In China, the choice of a go-between is nearly as crucial as the choice of the bride. In a village marriage, the go-between must negotiate and remember accurately and honestly all of the involved terms of the marriage settlement. She scours the countryside for a family of appropriate status and makes discrete inquiries among their neighbors, friends, and enemies about the health, character, virtue, and industry of the prospective bride. Few parents are so bereft of friends and relatives that they cannot make an additional private set of enquiries about the bride and her family, but it is on the go-between's researches that most decisions are based. Her honesty must be unquestionable, her ability to analyze character infallible, her experience extensive, and above all else, her loyalty to the young man's family must be firmly and irrevocably established. She must, nonetheless, seem equally trustworthy to the family of the bride, giving them the impression that she is their ally, working for their interests. This is the ideal go-between and here Lim Han-ci chose without error. Ng Kui-lian was at that time in her middle sixties and had been an active and highly successful go-between for over twenty years. She lived no more than 100 yards from the Lims, and her family had lived in Peihotien for at least two generations before her birth. Her sons had prospered and had been assisted toward their prosperity by the Lims. They still consult with Lim Chieng·cua and Lim A·bok on a variety of subjects, ranging from insecticides to investments. A bride's family could not bribe Ng Kui·lian to hide their daughter's defects until after the final ceremony, or raise the bride price and lower the dowry. This go·between's loyalty was unquestionable.

Unfortunately, Lim Han·ci's choice of a bride was not as astute as his choice of a go·between. In deciding among the several girls that Ng Kui·lian presented for his approval, he broke a fundamental rule. Chui·ieng was attractive, intelligent, healthy, and of the right age for his son. She was reputed to be strong·minded, but no rumor of really bad behavior was found among her neighbors. She was an adopted daughter but had been adopted into a childless family, so there was no suspicion that she was being rejected as an unsuitable bride for the son of that family. She did not have a reputation for skill in the domestic arts, but this was not at all unusual for young women from families of modestly comfortable means. Many mothers consider their permissive treatment of their daughters a kindness, at the same time cursing their new daughters·in·law for the slack upbringing that makes them so useless in their marital homes. But this was a minor fault. The major fault was one that Lim Han·ci foolishly chose to disregard. Chui·ieng was born into an urban family far wealthier than the Lims, and adopted into a family which was perceptibly better off than the Lims. When his go·between pointed this out as a serious disadvantage, Lim Han·ci made an error of pride. The house of Lim had risen so far in his lifetime that his perspective blurred. When Chieng·cua caught sight of the handsome girl and indicated his approval to his father, the decision was made. Lim Han·ci dismissed the long·accepted custom that wives should be selected from families whose status was the same or slightly inferior to their husband's. It was a decision he and the rest of the family regretted from the day Chui·ieng entered the house. She persistently brought to everyone's mind, both intentionally and through ignorance, the reason for this rule of marriage. Although not accustomed to a life of luxury, she was used to more comforts than she found with the Lims. She did not consider the price of a bus ticket to the next town a serious expenditure. The closest she had come to agriculture was in picking flowers, but the Lims expected her help, albeit minimally, during the rush periods of harvest. Although she knew she would have to learn to cook for a large family, her intense pride prevented her from taking gruff corrections humbly. In her own home, she had learned to dictate to a young servant, to express any frustration with a display of anger that confused her more even-tempered parents and made the servant scurry. Worst of all for Lim Han-ci, her dissatisfaction quickly turned to scorn for the family into which she had married. She became the only adult in the family who did not take seriously their almost fanatic desire to preserve the family's dignity and good name. She looked down on them as inferiors and saw no good name to be preserved. Her excessive evaluation of her own worth prevented her from making any friends in the village and consequently prevented her from damaging the family with idle gossip, but she was totally unwilling to control her strong feelings when their public display could only injure the family in the eyes of its neighbors. To her, they had nothing to lose.

When I came to live with the Lim family, Lim Chui-ieng had been married for seventeen years and had borne her husband six children. Most village women after this length of time visit their natal homes only rarely and have thoroughly, if not peacefully, identified with the family of their husbands and their children. Lim Chui-ieng had not made this adjustment. Family secrets, the very existence of which other family members denied, were fair topics of conversation for Chui-ieng. In her loneliness, she seized upon my interpreter as a confidante, telling her at every opportunity of the tragedy that was her life, a tragedy culminating in her marriage to Lim Chieng-cua. Even though her stories are distorted and biased in her own favor, they show what a disrupting effect she has had on the Lim family.

"I was adopted," she said, "when I was four or five months old. My father's older brother was a very well-known man, and my family was very particular about only giving daughters to a family who had sons for them to marry. My grandmother was very strict, and she would only let each of her three sons keep one daughter. They had to give the rest away.

"My foster mother and father quarreled a great deal from the time they were married, and so they didn't have any children. His mother decided that it would be a good idea to adopt a child for them. She thought that once they had a child they wouldn't fight anymore. She had just borne a baby girl herself, so she gave her away and adopted me to drink her milk. She wanted to get a baby so badly that she lied to my parents and told them they already had a son. Then, when the go-between came, she borrowed a neighbor's boy and said it was the son I was to marry.

"When my real parents found out the truth, they said they were going to burn the go-between with firecrackers when she came to get her money. She didn't dare to come. My uncle was very proud and had a great deal of influence, so she didn't dare say anything about it.

"If I hadn't been tricked away like that, I wouldn't be where I am now and have such a bad life. All my sisters married their foster brothers and they are all very rich and very happy now. My family always gave their daughters to families with sons. It saved them the trouble of having to marry the girls out themselves, and the girls made respectable marriages. It does not look good for an adopted daughter to marry out of her family no matter what. People will say, 'Oh, that woman married twice!' [The implication is that her first marriage occurs upon adoption.]

"When they found out how they had been tricked, my uncle came to my foster parents house to get me back. He even brought something to carry me home in, but when he got there and saw how much everyone liked me and how well they were treating me, he decided to let me stay. I guess he just decided that was my fate.

"But really, the people in my foster family liked me very much. The people who lived around there all called me 'the aristocrat of the adopted daughters.' From the time I was adopted until I married, I never had to cook or do much else. I helped to take care of the younger children and did a little housework, but that was all. My father and mother and grandmother all liked me very much and were very good to me.

"Five years after I was adopted, my foster mother had her first child. Until then I was the only child in the family and could do whatever I wanted. I slept with my grandmother and she petted me each night until I went to sleep. It was the same until I married. No matter how late it was, I would wait for my grandmother before I would go to bed. I was afraid to go to sleep by myself. That was because they tricked my parents that way and adopted me so young. All of my sisters and my father's brother's daughters weren't adopted until they were three years old.

"I go to visit my natal family and my foster family very often."

Of her marriage Lim Chui-ieng told me: "She [probably the go-between] came to talk about a marriage when I was nineteen, but I said I didn't want to get married. I still didn't want to get married when I was twenty-three, but my parents made me do it. It was all because of my parents. I knew about this family and I didn't want to marry into it. It is better the way they do it now—it is better to pick out your husband yourself because then you can get along together. See how it is with me. I didn't want this marriage and I was right. We don't get along at all. He is always going *peng, peng, peng* [the sound used to denote scolding]. There is nothing good about an arranged marriage. The very most you can do is visit your parents now and then and say, 'I didn't want to marry him and you made me do it so now you are responsible for my suffering.' But when I was married, all of the marriages were arranged by the parents. And that is the stupidest thing in the world.

"I was only 19 when they came to talk about this marriage. I wouldn't do it, and my grandmother wouldn't make me do it. She didn't like the things she heard about the Lims either. But three years later my mother and her husband's elder brother's wife went ahead and arranged this marriage. Every time I go home, I complain to them that they gave me a sad, hard life."

I pointed out to Chui-ieng that I often see her sitting with her husband whispering to him about various things and she answered indignantly, "Oh you. You are so dumb. He beats me all the time because we get along so well, is that why? You don't know how hard I had to work when I first married into this family. I even had to go out and work in the fields with the rest of them. And all the time he is scolding . . ."

My assistant, whose honesty at times overwhelms her diplomacy, suggested, "Well, he only hits you when something happens. He doesn't hit you just to amuse himself."

Chui-ieng could not deny the truth of this but asserted, "Yes, but I'll always remember it. I'll never forget it until I die. I'll always remember to bring it up and talk about it once in awhile."

Lim Chieng-cua and Chui-ieng have four boys and two girls. Their first born, Kim-hok, is a tall, handsome boy in his early teens. He has the long-boned body and the fine, thin features of his father's family. He also has their temperament and in him I fear it will be a handicap that it was not to the generations before him. Their strength and self-confidence show up in Kim-hok as stubborn arrogance. The smallest slight by one of his peers, intentional or accidental, demands a disproportionate retaliation. His temper is as violent as that of his father and grandfather, but unlike them his reason does not always return when it cools. He holds grudges far longer than most children his age. Old Lim Han-ci was in his last years when Kim-hok was born and he catered to the child's whims in a way that amazed his son and perplexed his two older grandchildren. With Lim A-pou's two children he had been only a little more lenient than he had with his own children, but when his second son presented him with a grandson he seemed to forget the lessons he had learned—he gave Kim-hok all the grandfatherly indulgence and protection from discipline that had cost him so much with his own eldest son, Lim Hue-lieng. If he had lived a few years longer, perhaps he might have used his influence over the boy to help Chieng-cua redirect his son's explosive nature into more creditable behavior. But, he died too soon, leaving Kim-hok with the imprint of his indulgence but not of his training.

If Chieng-cua were married to a woman with a quiet, gentle personality, such as his mother had, he could by the strength of his own character pass on much of his father's training. Instead he is married to a strong-minded woman who is constantly at war with him. Their children have become her weapons. This is not an uncommon state of affairs in a Chinese household. When a woman enters her husband's house, she comes as a stranger without friends or relatives. She has no status in that family until she bears a son, but even then the comfort of her declining years is not assured unless she can bind that son to her with the ties of gratitude and affection. Chinese society demands of a young man that he care for his aged father—if he does not he is an outcast in his home district and under suspicion everywhere else. The dictum also includes his aged mother, but women matter less in China. The social pressure in her behalf is not as great. To establish her claim, a Chinese mother depends not upon the sanctions of society, but on the ties she herself can create, the ties of emotion buried so deeply in the mind as to be ineradicable. The Taiwanese believe that after a boy reaches six or seven years of age, his father must withdraw and treat him sternly and without affection in order to maintain authority, respect, and obedience. If a woman's relations with her husband are not good, she can make excellent use of her husband's aloofness to increase her children's resentment of him and strengthen their ties to her. Even if she bears her husband no malice, she makes use of his cold sternness to protect her own future; she attempts to preserve her children's respect for their father, but she reserves their affection for herself.

Lim Chui-ieng is full of malice toward her husband and she uses every means available to her to both undermine her husband's authority and his children's respect for him. She allows Kim-hok to do as he pleases and even plots with him ways of getting around orders his father has issued to him. Except for frowns of disapproval and an occasional formal beating, Lim Chieng-cua has no tools left to him in training his son. Chui-ieng's scorn for the other members of the family has been conveyed to her children without hindrance. Masa, who is only five or six years older than Kim-hok, has always teased him and ordered him about, enforcing his orders with his superior strength. Had Masa's father been the head of the family rather than Kim-hok's, the younger boy might have borne his subjection more easily. Instead he developed an intense hatred for Masa that reached its peak one night when Kim-hok was nine or ten years old. Lim A-pou walked into her son's bedroom and found Kim-hok about to bury a knife in Masa's sleeping form. Even Kim-hok's mother was horrified by this incident.

Le-cu, a girl, was born when Kim-hok was about two years old. She is approaching adolescence now but without the clumsy selfconsciousness of American children. She runs with the grace of a forest animal and all of her movements, intense where her mother's are simply tense, are a joy to watch. She is quick to anger but within an hour she may be joking with the person at whom she was raging. Her mother allows her a freedom of expression that plainly shocks other village mothers. Neighbors who have girls her age regret their daughters' friendship with Le-cu because they fear she will lead them into unsuitable activities. Her peers consider her "fearless." She hates school and argues constantly with her mother about quitting. Most girls her age are burdened with the care of their younger siblings, making school a welcome respite, but Le-cu manages to avoid most responsibilities. I frequently saw her playing with her younger brothers and sisters and helping them, but more because it amused her than because it was expected of her. They bring to her their broken toys and bruised knees rather than going to their impatient mother.

Thiam-hok, Lim Chieng-cua's third child and second son, is an unusual Lim. He is quiet, slight of build, and slow to anger. He is immensely popular and is included in whatever game is being played, but he rarely takes the lead and never seems to expect it. He is content to think up new variations on old games and let the others carry them out. Thiam-hok often sits alone daydreaming or perhaps thinking. I have seen this kind of behavior in other village children, children suffering from the debilitation of frequent illness and inade-quate diet, but with Thiam-hok one senses activity behind his with-drawn face. Several times I have come upon him hiding in a quiet corner, hunched over a piece of paper. Before he could conceal it, I saw that he was sketching with a stubby pencil and sketching with a certain amount of talent. My sincere praise did nothing to lessen his embarrassment—I had stumbled into what he evidently considered a secret, sinful pleasure. I later heard his siblings and even his mother teasing him about his pictures, but he did not abandon the activity. He only became more circumspect. To the initial amusement of his par-ents, he announced at the age of eight that he would no longer eat any form of meat, including vegetables fried in pig fat, a Taiwanese fam-ily's most common source of animal protein. He wished to live the life of a Buddhist. Lim Chui-ieng humored him for a few weeks, but when it became clear that he was serious, she forced him to return to normal eating habits for fear of damage to his already delicate consti-tution. He finally submitted, although he vowed to return to the stern discipline of Buddhism when he was fully grown. In determination he is definitely a Lim, but in him, the family character is taking a curious twist.

Lim Chieng-cua's fourth child and third son is my favorite. Even the most persistent teasing of his elder siblings fails to ruffle Kui-hok's good humor. He has none of Thaim-hok's dreaminess but his face nearly always has a shy smile on it. He was not yet in school when I lived with his family, so I saw a good deal of him. He came to our office nearly every day to collect curly pencil shavings which he dis-tributed to all of his friends. Although he is not beyond the usual teasing of younger siblings, he always gives in when they show signs of tears and leaves if they begin to vent their rage on him. Either his emotions burn with a cooler flame or he has already found a method for controlling them. One day when I was walking along a path I found him energetically slashing the tops off some long grass with a toy wooden sword. I asked conversationally what he was doing and he said, "Cutting off heads." I fumbled linguistically and quite by acci-dent blurted out, "Whose?" He promptly gave me the name of Lim A-bok's young son, the tiny family tyrant, smiled, and ran off to join a nearby ball game. Unlike any of his brothers and sisters, Kui-hok openly adores his father. Even the adults are amused by his practice of hoarding any treats that come his way to share with his father. He is shy, particularly with us, but not so shy that he wouldn't occasionally slip his hand into my husband's when they happened to be going in the same direction.

Lim Chui-ieng now uses her older children as substitutes for the adult friends she has been unable or unwilling to make in the village, but as infants she did not find the solace in them that many unhappy wives do. After the first two, she was unable to produce sufficient milk and had to rely on powdered milk and local substitutes such as rice gruel and soy milk. She complains of the work they cause her, and she complains of the bad effect her pregnancies have had on her health. After the birth of Kui-hok, Lim Chieng-cua made an extraordinary suggestion for a Chinese husband. He told his wife to have an hysterectomy, the only means of birth control considered reliable at that time by the Taiwanese. Most men, even men considerably poorer than Lim Chieng-cua, are unwilling to limit the size of their families. The number of sons a man has is a great source of pride. An old man told me, "People here don't ask how much money you have. They ask how many sons you have." Perhaps the fact that Lim Chieng-cua had three sons and was seriously concerned about Taiwan's population problems prompted his suggestion to his wife. And perhaps he was looking at the more personal future of his family. If his three sons as adults could not live in harmony under the leadership of the eldest, their share of the family property would be divided in three portions. A three-way division of Lim Chieng-cua's half of the family estate would make small portions and more sons with even smaller shares would land each of them back close to where old Lim Han-ci had begun. Lim Chieng-cua may also have been worried about his wife's health although to me she looked stronger than most of her neighbors. Perhaps he was just tired of her complaints.

Out of fear, Lim Chui-ieng delayed the operation until after the birth of two more children. Lim Chieng-cua remarked to me once that it would have been a great blessing to everyone if she had gone when he first suggested it. The fifth child, Bieng-cu, is an ugly, sulky little girl. Her habitual expression is one of barely repressed anger. She has not yet the courage to express her feelings in attacks on her peers so she resorts to attacks on their possessions, their smaller siblings, or to vicious cursing from a safe distance. She is disliked by most of the village children and finds her only companionship with Tan A-hong's youngest daughter. Chai-ngo is gradually rejecting her as she becomes better acquainted in the village, leaving Bieng-cu to her own devices which consist mainly of tormenting the last born of Lim Chieng-cua's children, Cin-hok. When I left the village, Cin-hok was the four-year-old stereotype of all last-born boys in Chinese families. He acts much younger than his age and takes full advantage of his position. He cries more than any child I have ever known, but his tears can be turned on and off at will. To stop them one need only comply with the demand that started them, and that is exactly what everyone in the family does. What A-bok's young son achieves with insolent charm, Cin-hok gets with long, sullen crying. Both Bieng-cu and Cin-hok are lacking in the family good looks. They resemble neither parent but are square, stocky-looking peasants.

After Cin-hok's birth, Lim Chui-ieng entered a hospital and had an hysterectomy. When she left the hospital she went to her adoptive parents' home and informed them that she never intended to step foot in her husband's house again. I have no idea what plans she had for supporting herself, but after a few weeks her foster brothers told her firmly that she must return to her husband. Even if she believed them far superior to her husband's family, they could not afford to support another man's wife for the rest of her life. Poor Chui-ieng's last attempt to reject her "fate" ran head on into reality. Personally, I question the sincerity of her avowed intention of severing her relations with the Lim family. I am more inclined to believe it was just another attempt to bring trouble and humiliation upon what she considered the unjustifiably proud head of her husband. She returned to him and her children just over a month after her operation.

chapter 11

NARROW HEARTS

According to Lim Chui-ieng, all of her unhappiness stems from some-one's ill use of her. In adult life that someone has been Lim Chieng-cua. Chui-ieng has chosen to focus on her husband's mistresses as the source of most of her troubles. Romantic love is considered irrelevant to marriage in China, and Chui-ieng had not even met her husband before her marriage, let alone seen enough of him to love him. None-theless, she felt insulted and threatened by the extra-marital activities he engaged in from the early years of their union. Her childhood, unusual for an adopted daughter, had not taught her the rewards of submission or the pretense of submission, but had accustomed her to being the center of large and small storms, many of them brought on by her displays of temper. In the Lim family tempers were a speciality and Chui-ieng's little displays caused only looks of disapproval. She had expected trouble in her new home, indeed her parents had warned her repeatedly that she would have to mend her ways when she mar-ried, but she had not expected to be ignored. I don't think it had ever occurred to her that she might not be able to control her husband as easily as she had controlled her foster parents.

Chui-ieng's failure made her frantic, but she was helpless. She could mask her despair with scorn, but the only reasonable criticism she could make of her husband was that the money he spent on mis-tresses would ruin the family. "It is not because my heart is narrow that I argue with my husband. It is because I want to save my family. If he spends all the money on girlfriends, what are my children to do? We aren't like Lim A-pou and her sons who only eat the rice in the middle of the pan [i.e. don't have to worry where it is coming from]. When my children's father has a girlfriend he takes her to movies and to restaurants, gambling and buying wine. They take friends along too, but he is the one who pays. And I? I have to ask for money like a beggar."

Lim Chieng-cua's neighbors look upon his affairs as quite natural to a man of his position and income. A wife's function is to bear children, raise them, and care for their home. Only the recent incursions of Western romanticism have encouraged the younger generations to look for something more in the marital relationship. Men who can afford it have always sought companionship outside their homes. If a man cannot afford these pleasures but takes them anyway, he is frowned upon by his neighbors and relatives—not for the injury he does his wife (for indeed there is no injury if he provides her and her children with a home and food), but for the injury to his ancestors and descendants whose property it is that he squanders.

According to his neighbors, Lim Chieng-cua chose his entertainment with moderation and in accordance with his income. A well-respected widow in the village who had been a good friend of Lim Chieng-cua's parents told me, "Lim Chieng-cua and his wife have gradually begun to get along better since his father died and left him to manage everything alone. Before then Chieng-cua had more time and so he always had a mistress. He could make a lot of money and so naturally he had girlfriends. His wife was always following him, trying to catch him with some woman. Whenever he went out, she would sneak along behind and then come back and tell his parents. When he came home, Lim Chieng-cua would politely say he had been to such and such a place on business, and then his wife would jump in and say exactly where he had been, with all the times and people listed. She embarrassed the old father and this made Chieng-cua mad. They quarreled every day. Lim Han-ci always told her, 'Let him alone. Don't always argue with him and you won't get beaten.' "

Because of their status in Peihotien, everything the Lims do, from the way they arrange their family altar to Lim Chieng-cua's business dealings, is of interest to their neighbors. Few people have the courage to openly question Lim Han-ci, Lim Chieng-cua, or, for that matter, even Lim A-pou about the activities of their household, but Lim Chui-ieng's recurrent indiscretions provide the village with much to discuss. She is too proud to have a confidante in the village or even a friend, but her pride did not prevent her from tracking her husband and quarreling with him in public. One might expect Lim Chieng-cua's less affluent neighbors to feel a certain amount of jealousy, but the stories they told me of his extra-marital activities are curiously loyal—vindictive only when they touch upon the behavior of his wife, the outsider. Chui-ieng's life is almost as bitter as she describes it, but the villagers believe she brought it on herself.

When we came to live with the family, Lim Chieng-cua had not kept a mistress for some time. Chui-ieng occasionally nagged her husband about past infidelities, but in general, relations between them were tranquil. Lim Chieng-cua's most recent affair, and the one which still seemed to worry his wife, was his liaison with Lau Kim-chiok, the adopted daughter of one of his neighbors. Lim A-pou told me, "A few years ago Lim Chieng-cua had a mistress here in the village. She was a prostitute who was living just then with a man who worked nights in the winery. I know she wasn't married to this man because I saw her police book and his name wasn't in it.

"Both Lim Chieng-cua and his wife have hot tempers and they have quarreled from the day they married. She would never just accept his having a mistress or try to find some peaceful means of getting him to stay home at night. Instead, she used to go to the woman's house at night and beat on the doors and make a lot of noise. One night she even broke a window in the house. This really made my brother mad. She ran home and hid in my room. My father was still alive then, but that night he was disgusted and said he wouldn't interfere any more. Lim Chieng-cua tried to break down the door of the room to get at his wife, and I'm sure he would have killed her if my son hadn't pulled him away and calmed things down.

"Then in the middle of the night he had to go and find a workman to repair the window in that woman's house so the man she was living with wouldn't find out what was going on.

"Not long after this both the man and woman got put into jail for using narcotics. His sentence was a very long one because he had quarreled with some powerful *lo mua* before he got caught. She was given a sentence of three and a half years. She should be getting out soon now."

When Lau Kim-chiok was released, she returned to her mother's home in the village. Friends and neighbors came to see her, both to welcome her home and out of curiosity. Lim Chieng-cua who was in Taipei on business didn't return to the village until late in the evening, but when he did, he also went to pay his respects to his former mistress. According to my interpreter, who was also there, he was simply another well-wisher. Needless to say, his wife did not accept his visit as a casual courtesy. Before long she too turned up at Lau Kim-chiok's party in search of her husband. He ordered her to leave and she did, but when he returned home hard words were exchanged.

My interpreter heard Chui-ieng crying in our kitchen and while trying to calm her, listened to her expressions of misery. "That stinking prostitute is home. She never lets my family live in peace. He [Lim Chieng-cua] went to see her the minute he heard she was back. He couldn't even wait for one night. That Hakka woman! [Lau Kim-chiok may have been adopted from Hakka parents, but the Taiwanese often use this as an insulting curse, the assumption being that Hakka are bad-hearted and generally low in morality]. She is most able to tempt people. She is full of sweet talk and honey. And he always listens to her temptings! The mosquito net was already set up when I got there and I'm sure he was about to get in bed with her. He hits me because of her and that is what has made me so sickly. I wasn't that way before.

"You don't know how fierce that prostitute is. How thick the skin on her face is! [i.e., you can't insult her.] Even worse, the family in the next lane are her allies. Before she went to jail, if my husband spent an evening at home, that prostitute would send them to come and call him out. Then five or six of them would go to see a play or eat and drink and my husband would pay for it all. This is a good chance for them now that she is back. They will be sure to come calling him out now just like before."

Lim A-pou made little effort to hide her amusement at her sister-in-law's predicament and at her behavior. "That woman's heart is too narrow. She should wait for awhile and see if they go back together again. Then she can go cause trouble if she wants to. Yesterday was her first day back and lots of people went to see her. Why doesn't Chui-ieng think before she runs out scolding. No wonder everybody knows all about it. I was already asleep last night so I didn't know anything about their fight, but early this morning it was all over the village. A long time ago I said that as soon as Lau Kim-chiok came back we'd have a good play to see. It was true. And on the first day!"

During the next few days I noticed some very peculiar behavior on the part of Lim Chieng-cua's older children. Uusally they were out of the house most of the day, coming in for meals or snacks or to pick up a ball. Now they seemed to be in and out of the house constantly,

holding whispered conferences with their mother and then disappearing again. And one evening when Lim Chieng-cua didn't return at his
usual time for dinner, Kui-hok asked, with tears running down his
face, "Where is father? Has he gone away?" Chui-ieng was using her
children to spy on their father. She had told them that he might run
away with another woman and if he did they would be abandoned to
starve. Chui-ieng knew perfectly well that her husband would do nothing so absurd, but by convincing his children of the possibility she
could both strengthen their ties to herself and keep a watchful eye on
her husband.

Early in her career Lau Kim-chiok, like most prostitutes,
adopted a daughter to support her when she was no longer pretty
enough to work. During Kim-chiok's imprisonment, the daughter
stayed with various relatives and finally came to live with her maternal grandmother in Peihotien. With the hope of at least delaying her
entrance into her mother's profession, Lim Chieng-cua gave the girl a
job in his factory. Lau Bit had been working there for quite some time
when her mother returned to the village. Two or three weeks after
Lau Kim-chiok's release from prison, Lau Bit was visited in the factory
by Le-cu, Lim Chieng-cua's eldest daughter. By this time the anxiety
Chui-ieng had aroused in her children was beginning to fade and their
spying had become a game. Le-cu, finding her father absent from the
factory, tried to pick a quarrel with Kim-chiok's daughter. Lau Bit
was several years older than Le-cu and much more conscious of the
seriousness of life. Le-cu taunted her about her mother's profession,
cursed her on general principles, and ordered her out of the factory.
Lau Bit left in tears, humiliated before the other factory girls who
watched round-eyed and fearful. Le-cu then went home to brag to her
mother of her clever deed. Chui-ieng was amused and cruelly pleased
by the story, but at the same time she realized that this was going to
cause no end of trouble. She immediately sent her daughter off to stay
with relatives in Lungyen. Her precautions were justified. When Lim
Chieng-cua returned to the factory and heard what had occurred in
his absence, he was furious. He went to his wife to ask his daughter's
whereabouts, telling her explicitly that he intended to beat the girl to
death when he found her. Chui-ieng told him calmly enough that she
had sent the girl to stay with relatives, but she could not refrain from
defending her child's indefensible behavior. One thing led to another
and Chui-ieng soon turned to her usual tirade against Lau Kim-chiok
and her family, accusing Lim Chieng-cua of treating "a prostitute's

bastards" better than his own children. This was too much. Lim Chieng-cua struck his wife a heavy blow across the mouth. She ran into the courtyard but he followed her, grabbing a heavy scaling pole as he went. Fortunately, A-bok was moving sacks of rice in the yard and pinned his uncle's arms before he could strike her. Instead of leaving, Chui-ieng turned back to attack her tightly-held husband. A-bok had to call Masa to pull Chui-ieng away. She then ran out of the house. The uproar brought the whole family out of the house, and the children were whimpering with fear. Lim Chieng-cua turned from his nephews without a word and disappeared into his bedroom. A-bok's young son, more curious than frightened, demanded of his father in a loud, clear voice, "Why were you fighting with Uncle?" Although his father insisted gruffly and repeatedly that they had not been fighting, his mother, characteristically, began to giggle. A-bok shouted at her to get back to work, and the others returned to the house. Tan Chun-ieng was home that evening and it was she who took over the care of Lim Chui-ieng's children, seeing to their baths and getting them into bed. Lim A-pou and her daughter-in-law, the latter probably under strict orders since basically she is a kind girl, completely ignored the frightened and tearful children. The youngest wandered around the house pathetically asking anyone who would listen, "Was Momma getting a spanking? Have you seen my Momma?" It was not the feared father who had abandoned them, but their beloved mother. Long after the house was usually quiet, I heard sobs coming from the children's sleeping room.

Lim Chui-ieng went to the only refuge she had in the village, the home of Ng Kui-lian, the go-between for her marriage. There she borrowed enough money to get her to relatives and left the village at once. A little over an hour after the quarrel, I heard the clump, clump of old Ng Kui-lian's cane aggressively announcing her progress through the house. Her status as the original go-between gave her the right and indeed the obligation to act as peace-maker in the present crisis. Her status as an old lady gave her the right to speak her mind to both parties. After soundly scolding Lim Chieng-cua for interrupting her late afternoon nap, she demanded full details of the quarrel. He spoke frankly and her comments were equally frank. They talked for the better part of an hour before the old woman was satisfied that both had been, as she suspected all along, in the wrong. With that she left, intending to put things back together the following day.

Much to my surprise, Lim Chui-ieng returned to the house the next morning accompanied by her father's elder sister, a tiny, trim old lady dressed in black. Instead of summoning Ng Kui-lian, who should have been present at any negotiations between the two, Chui-ieng informed her husband that she was leaving the family permanently. I cannot imagine what reaction she expected from her husband, but from her subsequent behavior it is clear that she didn't expect what she received. Lim Chieng-cua agreed readily and said he would send someone immediately to summon the police that they might remove her name from the household registration and issue her a new police book. After a stunned silence, Chui-ieng threw all her good sense to the winds and with the biting sarcasm that has cost her so much happiness said, "That will be fine, won't it? You will really be a famous man now." She planted her final taunt with venom. "Yes, everyone will talk about how great the Lim family is now." The aunt, shocked less by her niece's outburst than by the dark red color appearing on Lim Chieng-cua's face, made an attempt to avert what was to come. She shouted at her niece, "Look at his face! You know his health isn't good. It isn't good for his health to get so angry!" But she was too late. In a frenzy, Lim Chieng-cua beat his wife about the head, grabbed her by the hair, and threw her to the cement floor where he punished her brutally with his feet. The aunt was frozen in horror and A-bok and his family were long ago at work in the fields. I had to abandon my anthropological immunity and participate in some direct foreign intervention. Lim Chieng-cua was literally shaking with rage when he left the room—his arms were jerking uncontrollably. The aunt's first statement when her tongue thawed was a typical Taiwanese reaction to someone's physical injury. She began to scold Chui-ieng.

By the time her foster mother arrived that afternoon, Chui-ieng's right eye was swollen closed and her ear and the side of her head were discolored with bruises and clotted blood. As soon as she saw her, the mother began to cry, "It's all my fault. It's all my fault. Oh, to see my daughter like this! Your grandmother and your father said that we shouldn't marry you to a man with such a bad temper, but I wanted this marriage. It is all my fault!"

Chui-ieng replied by begging her mother to take her home. "If I stay here he will kill me. He will kill me, I know it. He said he would kill our daughter." The rest of that day and all of the next a parade of people passed through Chui-ieng's bedroom, and streams of curious neighbors found excuses to stop in the family kitchen to catch up on the latest details. As Masa scornfully commented, "If two ants had a fight, everyone in this village would know about it an hour later." A doctor came to give Chui-ieng an injection of penicillin, the local medical people's prescription for all manner of ills, and, of course, there was a large delegation of Chui-ieng's relatives, including her foster father, her sister, one of her foster father's brothers, and several other people whom I could not identify. Except for her mother, who probably would have agreed to take her daughter home, these people were primarily concerned to see that the quarrel reached an amicable settlement. The mistress of ceremonies in all these proceedings was Ng Kui-lian. With her stick and old-fashioned hand warmer, she hobbled about the house with surprising speed for a woman whose feet have been bound for 80 years. She scolded, cajoled, sympa-thized, threatened, and within a few hours settled the matter, not amicably perhaps, but inevitably. I do not know all she said to Chui-ieng except that she assured her that if her husband ever hit her again, she herself would beat him up, but I was present when she made Lim Chieng-cua promise that he would not beat his wife again and that he would not beat his daughter when she came home. When she approached him, he was talking to two women from Tapu who had the misfortune that day to come to visit Chui-ieng about the affairs of some distant relative. The presence of these two strangers did not inhibit Ng Kui-lian in the least. In fact, she seemed to take advantage of their presence as a means of putting the whole situation on record with unprejudiced outsiders, repeating for them the whole history of the quarrel. She was particularly explicit in enumerating the cuts Lim Chieng-cua had inflicted and the extent to which his wife's face and body were bruised. Even Lim Chieng-cua's sophistica-tion could not withstand the sharp, clinical tongue of Ng Kui-lian. He was writhing with embarrassment, glancing several times toward me as if to say, "How can you argue with an eighty-five-year-old woman?" His only defense was one brief comment. "She knows I have a bad temper and she knows that this subject makes me angry. She brings it up anyway." The next day Lim Chieng-cua made a special trip to Tapu to buy his wife some soft rice cakes. She was having difficulty chewing. When he returned, he took them into her himself, finally breaking his silence with a comment which was proba-bly meant to be sympathetic. "You have bad luck, woman."

Le-cu, the cause of all the trouble, did not return for several days but was finally summoned by her mother when it became apparent that Lim A-pou had no intention of departing from the established cycle of responsibility for cooking. Many men make a hobby of cooking, displaying their special skills at banquets and the like. We often savored some of Lim Chieng-cua's specialties, but in this situation it would have been impossible for him to step into the breach for even one meal, serving his nephews and children. Instead, his eldest son managed, and managed quite well, until his sister returned to assist him. To my knowledge, no words were exchanged between daughter and father, but one look at her mother probably was punishment enough. I do not imagine that Chui-ieng passed up this opportunity to tell Le-cu what she had suffered on her behalf. For several weeks Le-cu was a model daughter, but she avoided her father whenever possible.

By the time Lim Chui-ieng was moving around the house again, Lau Kim-chiok had gotten a job in a brothel in Wanhua and came back to the village once a month, if then. After a few months she formed one of the semi-permanent liaisons which makes a prostitute's life more bearable and sent for her daughter to live with her. Lau Bit never returned to work in the factory. Not long after, I noticed a gayly dressed young woman, rather heavily rouged, visiting Lau Kim-chiok's mother. My interpreter, amused that I did not recognize her, said that this was Lau Bit. She couldn't have been much over sixteen, but, as with so many young prostitutes, her youth disappeared with her innocence. Just before I left the village, I heard that Lau Bit had had her first abortion.

Relations between Lim Chieng-cua and his wife improved considerably after the crisis of Lau Kim-chiok's return. Although Lim Chieng-cua did not appear any more attentive than usual, I think his wife at last realized that among other things, her husband no longer cared for the responsibilities and expenses of the kind of entertainment he had enjoyed during his affair with Kim-chiok. He had not, in fact, for years, but Chui-ieng's outrage and jealousy prevented her from accepting this. She still complains about money and on occasion refers vaguely to past excesses, but she is more cautious now in her choice of words.

chapter 12

A
GIFT
OF
PRIDE

During the years we lived in Peihotien, my husband often turned to Lim Chieng-cua for solutions to the puzzles of village life. We were rarely disappointed by his suggestions. Many of the villagers, and even some of the educated men who are at ease in the classrooms of Taipei, shook their heads at our queries and gave us the thoughtless answer: "That's just the way it is done." Unlike his neighbors, Lim Chieng-cua enjoyed turning our questions over in his mind, often showing us that the error was in the question. We came to rely on his insights to send us down a more fruitful path in our search for understanding. It is not easy for a man who knows no other way of life, and who is a deeply involved participant in the life he knows, to step away from it, and to view it through an outsider's eyes. It is not easy, and it is often not pleasant, but for the Lims this has become a habit. Lim Chieng-cua is not the contemplative oriental so often described and so rarely seen. If he were, he would not have been of so much assistance to us, nor would his opinions have been so respected by his fellows. In the closed life of a Taiwanese village, the unusual quirks of a man's personality are accepted in the same way as a crippled leg: that's just the way he is. But, even the slightest suspicion of a more basic peculiarity—a man who questions the premises his neighbors call fact—leads to doubt and distrust. Because of the long hours he wasted talking with us, some of Lim Chieng-cua's neighbors wondered at his patience, others grew suspicious of his motives and ours, and the

more acute were uneasy at his obvious enjoyment of profitless discussion. Several times I saw this uneasiness in A-bok's face—a face and
perhaps a character more similar to Lim Han-ci's. Thiam-hok's
dreamy thoughts and his father's intellectual speculations suggest
weakness to the villager. And in a world where each meal can be
measured in hours of hard labor, they are a weakness. I hope his
neighbors concluded after our departure that the hours Lim Chieng-cua
wasted with us were only a modern variation of the hours he wasted
in the company of his mistresses.

I learned as much about the economics of the Lim household
and the Lim factory as I could hope to from a rational businessman. I
did not, however, learn anything from Lim Chieng-cua about the
problems that beset his family. We always talked around them, addressing ourselves to the general problem of why families cannot
achieve the ideal to which they all give lip service. My own notions
about the tensions that tear apart the extended family, many of them
based on simple observation of the Lims, were presented to the head
of the Lims and after some thought agreed to by him, but his examples were always in terms of some other family. There was a
reserve, often camouflaged by dry humor, that prevented me from
being as ruthless with personal questions as I was with other villagers.
Lim Chieng-cua held in his mind a clear picture of his family as he
wanted us to see it, and even if he thought we might be aware of the
flaws in this picture, he was not willing to discuss them. We were to
see a thriving, industrious farm family, supplementing its income with a
moderately lucrative home factory. Family members all contributed to the
common pot and received from the common pot, with final authority resting in the senior male, the head of the household. This was not a simple
game of presenting a shining face to the foreigner. We were only by-
standers. The more important audience was the village, the larger world
of Hotien, and distant but important relatives. It was for many years a
deception in which the entire family participated, with varying degrees
of willingness. It had not always been a deception.

Lim A-pou's dissatisfaction with the administration of the family
budget was more openly expressed during the second year of my stay
in the village, and in terms of simple facts, she was often justified in
her complaints. She refuses to accept, however, that a man who must
obtain custom from city businessmen must dress better than a farmer,
that school-age children require more clothes than children rolling

about the muddy courtyards of a country village. What are essentials for some family members are luxuries for others, and though painful for some, the family's needs must be evaluated dispassionately by the man who manages the family budget. When this man is also the one who requires what the others only want, the complication smacks of injustice. To Lim A-pou, it is a simple case of one half of the family working very hard and the other half living better, sweating less. Even a man with less intelligence than Lim Chieng-cua would have to recognize the inevitability of the future.

About one thing everyone in the family seems to agree: things were better when Lim Han-ci was alive. Lim A-pou's memories of how generously her foster father rewarded her for raising pigs have already been mentioned. Lim Chui-ieng amused me with a rather different version of the old man's generosity: "From the head of the village to its tail, Lim A-pou and her daughter-in-law say we don't give them money to spend and that they have to wait like children until New Year's to get anything new. Their words are more than two baskets of 100 jin each and include everything. From a good heart [i.e., to tell the truth], they don't have much money when there are no vegetables to sell, but when they harvest vegetables, you notice they seem to have quite a bit of money. That comes from somewhere. It isn't like when my husband's father was alive. He made them tell exactly how many jin they sold and what they got for each jin and he counted the money very carefully."

Even Lim Chieng-cua, coming closer to admitting to problems within the family than in any other interview, spoke with something more than nostalgia for the days when his father was the titular head of the household: "When my father was an old man, he turned over the management of the family to me. I would make the decisions and then ask for his approval. It was easier to manage the family in those days. Father's approval was a simple 'yes' and his disapproval a simple 'no,' and that was the way it was done. Now I must get the approval of Lim A-pou or A-bok."

I think if Lim Chieng-cua had been willing to speak freely about the tensions within his family, he would have cited the ambiguity of his position and of his authority as the source of the family's problems. If, like his father, he had complete control and responsibility for all decisions in the family, the content of his decisions might be questioned, but not his right to make them. The right of a father to make decisions affecting his adult children is assumed. Lim Chieng-cua, however, is not the father. He is only the eldest male of the family, and a second son at that. The widow of the eldest son—the son who under ordinary circumstances would be in Chieng-cua's position—is still alive and, moreover, now has a son who is contributing a full adult share to the family budget. Undoubtedly this ambiguity in the structure of the family influences the attitudes of Lim A-pou and her son, but Lim Chieng-cua differs from his father in more than position. Their ways of looking at life are quite different, and their expectations for their future, vastly different. Lim Han-ci expected little improvement in his economic circumstances and received much, but this did not change his daily behavior nor his future expectations. He still desired for himself and his family the same things he desired when he was eating sweet potatoes because he couldn't afford rice. Lim Chieng-cua, like an American, expects a great deal more economic improvement and orders his life in terms of it, shedding those things of the past that he can, without losing the respect of his neighbors, and taking on those bits of the future that he can afford, without causing his neighbors to talk. To Lim A-pou who does not wish to walk any other path than that of her father, who thinks of prosperity in terms of more elaborate feasts, larger land holdings, and bigger contributions to the temple, Lim Chieng-cua's handling of the family purse is fraught with disaster. To Lim A-bok who respects and understands both views but is still too unsure to choose, Lim Chieng-cua's authority is frustrating and unfair.

During the second year of our stay with the Lims, an attempt was made to adjust at least their economic disagreements and to forestall what seemed at that time the imminent division of their extended family. It was agreed that Lim A-bok and his mother would take control of the income from the family land and that out of this income they would provide all of the family's food. Whatever was left was theirs to spend as they saw fit. The income from the factory remained under the control of Lim Chieng-cua and he was responsible for all of the family's other needs, such as major purchases for the house, its repair, gifts for weddings, funerals, and the other social obligations of the family. To a non-Chinese, this separation of incomes seems not only reasonable but in the natural order. To the Lims and their neighbors, it was unusual. In Peihotien, if a family loses confidence in its manager, they either divide the family or make do with a poor manager. Neither of these alternatives was agreeable to the Lims. They were too proud to divide, and the tension was too great for them to continue as they were. They chose instead to innovate, to compromise on an untraditional but still acceptable solution. Economically, the family now had two decision makers, but it remained one family, cooking joint meals on one stove.

For many months things were peaceful in the house of Lim. Lim A-pou no longer had reason to complain that Lim Chui-ieng was secretly buying special food for her own children. And, Lim A-pou was now free to reinstate the special sacrifices to the ancestors on their own death and birth days. Almost immediately after the compromise was reached, she also resumed the bi-monthly offerings of food and incense. For many village families these are the only days of the month when they taste meat, but the Lims can afford to eat meat without the excuse of a ceremony. Lim Chieng-cua had abolished the ceremony because he considered buying the required three kinds of meat on one day wasteful. To Lim A-pou, it was a necessity.

Even their neighbors noticed the new atmosphere amongst the Lims. Some of them noted it grudgingly, and some with real pleasure. But one woman, a woman who sincerely wished the best for the Lims because of her long friendship with the older generations of the family, told me, "A family is supposed to be like that, like they are now. The people in that family are all very good to outsiders, but they can't seem to get along with themselves. I'm glad that things have improved, but I fear that they are just getting along in the face and not in the heart."

Unfortunately, this woman's wisdom could not be denied. There soon was a quarrel between Lim A-pou and Lim Chui-ieng that revealed how thin the appearance of harmony really was. Again the relations between A-bok and his uncle seemed strained.

Why didn't the family simply separate and go their own ways? What possible good could outweigh the stress and dissatisfaction of their joint life? My husband and I have thought about this a great deal in the years since we left Taiwan and, as with any human predicament, have come up with no single answer. There is no formula for human behavior that takes the pride of the Lims into account. The very fact that most village families divide their household within a few years after their sons marry was a strong incentive for the Lim family not to do so. A-bok's concern about his fields, that he must keep other people from saying of his family "they are just like us now" was typical of both his mother's and his uncle's attitude toward the kind of standards they should maintain in the eyes of their neighbors. But for Lim A-pou, the standards, if simpler, were certainly more rigid, and Lim Chieng-cua did not always behave in accordance with her standards.

Beyond this, there was still the influence of Lim Han-ci. Ancestral tablets occupy a prominent place in the homes of Peihotien, and given the stimulation of daily rituals, one might expect that memories of the dead occupy a prominent place in the thoughts of the living. But Lim Han-ci's influence on the lives of his descendants is something more than can be explained in terms of ancestor worship. My husband was particularly impressed by this on a day when he joined the family in a climb into the mountains behind Tapu to clean Lim Han-ci's grave. Although the entire family was present, it was not marked by the strain characteristic of their dealings with each other on every other day of the year. They were naturally somewhat hesitant about making jokes at one another's expense, so accustomed had they become to quarreling, but much to my husband's surprise, they all joined in on the fun of making jokes about the presence of a foreigner. Playing on the Chinese way of referring to all foreigners as "foreign ghosts," Lim Chieng-cua wondered what his father would think about their bringing a ghost to help clean his grave, and Lim A-bok laughingly suggested that since all of the people in the village called my husband Lim anyway, they might just introduce him as an adopted son. This kind of light-heartedness continued all through the day. If one had not known the family at home, it would be easy to think that no discord existed among them. Perhaps it would not be too far-fetched to imagine that on this one day when their thoughts were all turned toward Lim Han-ci, they were embarrassed to reveal even to themselves what had happened to his family since he had left them.

The day we left Peihotien, our pedi-cab bristling with suitcases and gifts, Lim A-pou and her sister-in-law, Lim Chui-ieng, stood together in the doorway of the house of Lim to bow farewell. The next day at the Taipei Airport, Lim Chieng-cua, confident and at ease in a well-tailored dark suit, wished us a good voyage and a speedy return. He was accompanied by his nephew, A-bok, looking uncomfortable in the suit he usually wore only at New Year, shifting his calloused, work-stained hands as though they were an embarrassing package. We took our leave of the descendants of old Lim Han-ci as they wished us to take it, carrying an image of a family given dignity and honor by remaining united where others had failed. People in China make no effort to remove the price tags from the gifts they give. The fact that we could calculate so closely the cost of the image the Lims wished to send with us only added to its value, for them and for us.

SEPARATE STOVES

A few months after our return to America, we received a letter from a friend who had recently visited the Lims. The price was too high, the innovation has failed. The Lims have divided their property and established independent households. Lim A-bok continues to cultivate all the family land, but he now works Lim Chieng-cua's share of the land as a tenant. The family remains in the same house. They continue to share the guest hall and to worship there together, but some of the doors connecting their apartments have been nailed closed. The final admission of defeat is the presence of a new kitchen in the back of the house: they have divided the stove.

Our physical presence in the house was obviously the last delay of the inevitable. With our rooms scattered as they were through the building, it would have been difficult to arrange an equitable division without disturbing our living arrangements and creating even more controversy over the terms of the property settlement. The Americans and their rent were part of the estate. No matter how much she desired the division, even Lim A-pou was unwilling to have it take place with the acrimony common to most family divisions. If there had to be a step down, it must be made with dignity. Perhaps they viewed those final months of waiting as a sacrifice to Lim Han-ci— that his hope for a united family of many generations living under one roof might be a reality somewhere, even if only in the minds of foreigners.

Essentially, the house of Lim is no more. From the point of view of their neighbors, the Lims are "just like us now." They have returned to the cycle of growth and division which is the Chinese farmer's compromise with an ideal. But, on the altar in their guest hall there remains the ancestral tablet of Lim Han-ci. The strength of his personality and of his memory held them together for many years. In the end, it was not enough.